Financial Freedom Blueprint

FINANCIAL FREEDOM BLUEPRINT

7 STEPS TO ACCELERATE YOUR PATH TO PROSPERITY

Angie,
Thank you
All the Best!

LOUIS LLANES

HOUNDSTOOTH PRESS

Financial Freedom Blueprint: 7 Steps to Accelerate Your Path to Prosperity

Hardcover ISBN: 978-1-5445-2607-2
Paperback ISBN: 978-1-5445-2606-5
eBook ISBN: 978-1-5445-2608-9

To my grandfather, who raised a large family, including my dad. His life and struggles give me the inspiration to be strong, the desire to be loyal to family, and the motivation to be resilient after setbacks.

In theory there is no difference between
theory and practice. In practice there is.
—Yogi Berra

Contents

Ahead of the Herd

1

The secret of change is to focus all of your energy, not on fighting the old, but on building the new.

—Socrates

When I got out of college in 1994, I quickly learned that following the established rules of Wall Street and the academic community can be hazardous to your investment performance. When I started my career as a professional investor, the stock market had started to roar higher, and investors saw back-to-back years of banner growth. The world was enamored with the internet and all things dot-com.

My finance training indoctrinated me with the common wisdom taught in business school and the Chartered Financial Analyst (CFA) curriculum. That wisdom asserted that you should focus your attention on trying to value companies and invest in stocks that had excellent valuation based on detailed fundamental analysis. This way of thinking is still the predominant method used on Wall Street today.

At first, this method worked very well in the market for me. But then something strange happened—something that was never taught in business school or the CFA curriculum. My stocks, which had great fundamentals, started heading down hard, while poor quality stocks with no earnings skyrocketed. This continued for a couple of years. My firm started losing assets as people began to move their money to mutual funds that were investing in everything dot-com. Investors were hypnotized by greed and throwing out the fundamentals. Many of the best, strictly fundamental managers saw their portfolios get slashed in value. In fact, Warren Buffett, one of the most famous value investors, saw his portfolio in Berkshire Hathaway crash in value, going down over 50 percent during this period of time. It was brutal.

Then, everything reversed. In the year 2000, all of the poor-quality dot-com stocks crashed while stocks with good fundamentals moved much higher. If you were a buy-and-hold index investor who followed the conventional wisdom, you would have suffered losses for well over a decade because most of your stocks would be invested in the companies that crashed!

I estimate that 80 percent of investors are following the established rules that were invented and promoted by Wall Street. I believe that investors will do much better if they step away from products sold to the masses. Mass-marketed products tend to water down your ability to generate solid, risk-adjusted returns. I also believe that investors should take a different approach than the buy-and-hold convention.

Instead, I support *not* conforming to the established rules that have been preached by the financial services industry, but to think independently based on a formula that I will introduce. I'm talking about changing your habits and not following the herd.

This is Not Your Parents' Economy

As I write this, in 2021, we are in a completely different economic and political environment. This world is nothing like that experienced by your father or your grandfather, and for that reason, the opportunities are completely different. We are making way for new innovation and leaving the old economy of the past behind.

What has changed? Much of the change is driven by technology and innovation. But what is more important is that the current change is affecting virtually all industries. But there are a couple of headwinds we must overcome: poor government management and social unrest. If I had to encapsulate it in a nutshell, these are the changes that will have the most significant impact on your future returns:

- enormous innovation spurred by technological developments in many industries
- huge debt issuance by governments and deficit spending around the world
- enormous increases in the money supply by global central banks in most developed countries

- a widening gap between the rich and the poor
- corrupt government behavior

The Bright Future

The world is experiencing an explosion in new companies with new products and services. It's an exciting time for investors, filled with opportunity. As technology has sped up, it is affecting virtually all sectors of the economy. This innovation will continue to lead to big winners and losers.

The goal is to be in a winning position during great periods of change.

While innovation is encouraging, unfortunately progress is threatened by

- irrational government spending;
- increasing regulation; and
- extreme political division.

Ten years ago, if someone would have told me that the United States would have as much debt and deficit spending as we have today, I would have said they were crazy. If ten years ago someone would have told me interest rates would be near 0 percent in the United States and negative in Europe, I would have said, "We must be entering a depression." If someone were to tell me that the election process in the United States was riddled with accusations of errors and corruption, I would have said, "That only happens in third-world countries—not the United States."

Yet, this is the economic and political backdrop we have today.

It will likely have long-term implications, making it more difficult for you to protect and grow your money the same way your parents did. The good news is you can overcome this and be a winner!

Be Aware of the Established Rules

Before I get into the key ways to win, let's talk about what most of the financial services industry is pitching to American investors and the established policies that they want you to follow. I have an intimate knowledge of how the system works. I learned about it firsthand while working for a large brokerage firm and a large bank as a portfolio manager. Our department managed billions of dollars for high-net-worth people. I advised many different types of investors ranging from mom-and-pops to CEOs of publicly-traded corporations.

One of the things I found out is that we had a tremendous number of resources and access to the best institutional research. Yet, when I looked at the results of our clients, they were lackluster. I was shaking my head all the time, asking, "Why is this happening?" I decided to roll up my sleeves and really began an effort to study the very best investors who did well. Here is the biggest secret I learned: the absolute best investors *break away* from the orthodox way of doing things.

Wall Street wants to sell packaged products that are cookie-cutter. You are at a great advantage because you can tune out Wall Street's pitch. Instead, you can be nimble by investing in future innovation, diversifying, and protecting yourself from unruly governments.

Avoid Products to the Masses

There are many advertisements by investment firms that say, "We care about you as an individual." Most of the time what's really going on behind the scenes is that they are promoting assembly-line portfolios and selling them through advisors who have no real experience making money in the markets.

This is the type of investing the masses are doing—cookie-cutter and watered down. I believe most investors should go back to basics. Step away from the investing habits of the 80 percent and *enter the realm of rational active management where your portfolio is free to invest in attractive opportunities without regard to how the indexes are invested.*

What exactly is the product that is being sold to the masses? It is basically a structured product that owns everything in a given market. It is massively diversified and invests in securities with very little discrimination. In this strategy, you own so many securities that your investments are exposed to the whims of the overall stock market.

They are implemented in exchange-traded funds, index funds, and other packaged products sold as active funds, but they are really "closet index funds." There is little to no customization for the economy or your personal situation. You may hear a salesperson say, "Look how low your fees are," but you're basically owning everything, and you are socializing your returns.

Low fees will not rescue you from a 50 percent bear market if you own the S&P 500 Index Fund.

Socialization of Returns

Now the truth of the matter is, statistically speaking, many packaged investment products have very little differentiation because they correlate highly with each other. This is particularly true with stock investments. In many cases, it can be proven that the correlation between these instruments, meaning how much they move up and down together, is approaching .80 to .90 much of the time. In other words, 80 to 90 percent of the variance moves together. This means that when an inevitable bear market happens, which is normal from time to time, most of your investments will fall in value. It also may take a longer time to recover. You think you are diversified because you have many funds, but you may not be because many of the stocks held in your portfolio are the same or very similar, and they are heavily invested in the largest companies. So, there's no differentiation between many products.

Unfortunately, most of the public is investing by the established rules—the rules set by Wall Street. I am going to propose you invest with a different formula that is more rational. Not in a static asset allocation portfolio with very little adjustment for conditions. Not in wrapped mutual funds with a lot of overlap. Not owning well over 1,000 securities in your stock portfolio.

Differentiate and Eliminate

To step away from the pack, you need to do something different.

- First, eliminate those investments that are part of the stagnant past, and put more of your capital into investments that are part of a growing future.

- Second, *adequately* diversify, but do not *excessively* diversify. Diversification is about balancing your risk. You should not own so many investments that none of them can make solid profits for you, but at the same time, don't overconcentrate in a single investment or theme that can ruin your financial future.

- Third, use active risk management. This is done by predefining your risk before taking each investment and sizing your positions to limit the risk to your portfolio. This requires investors to exit investments that are not working and hold on to your winners.

If you follow these principles, you have an opportunity to protect capital and still be invested for growth. The objective is *not* to beat the S&P 500, but to deliver competitive returns that can beat taxes and inflation, with manageable risks that let you sleep at night.

Selective Holdings and a Plan to Protect Capital

As an individual investor, you could own the individual stocks, but in a smart way because you balance diversification with concentration. Compare the three principles outlined above to what the financial services industry tells you to do. They tell you that you need to buy and hold the indexes, you need to buy an investment for the long haul and hold it. I do believe that long-term investments are the best; the difference is how you determine *which* investments to hold longer term. Because if you hold *everything* long-term, there is a simple truth: you will take on significant risk, particularly if you succumb to indiscriminate buy-and-hold in volatile investments like stocks, real estate, or other hard assets.

A way to improve your risk-adjusted returns is to manage your downside and hold your winners so they can be free to earn more profits. In other words, you have a plan to make more money when you are right, and lose less when you are wrong. This is called *asymmetry*. This requires a sound position-sizing method to determine how much you are going to put into your investments. It also requires an entry and exit method for your timing. These are not the tactics the financial services industry is telling you to use.

Bright Future versus Stodgy Past

I have created a framework called the *ADP Criteria* to help identify companies that are the best to consider for investment. The "A" stands for *adaptability*. Companies that can be more adaptive to changes in innovation are more likely to be good investments. The "D" stands for *desirability*. How desirable are the company's products or services now and in the future? The "P" stands for *profitability*. How profitable can the company's business model be?

A company is considered adaptive if they can thrive when the industry has rapid change. I learned about the importance of adaptability in my first finance job as a financial analyst intern at Intellogic Trace, a publicly-traded technology service firm that was a spin-off of Datapoint. Intellogic Trace had large government contracts selling and servicing mainframe computers. I was in the corporate financial planning division, interacting with all the financial departments in the firm. We needed to talk to all the finance departments because our job was to forecast financial statements and help the chief financial officer make decisions.

My first task was to analyze the profitability of divisions across the country. But little did I know, as a young analyst who was green, rapid change was about to kill the business. The personal computer was becoming more powerful and cheaper to run than mainframes. As a result, there was less need for mainframes as the PC took over. This suddenly left Intellogic Trace with large inventories and parts that were obsolete. News came out that huge government contracts, which were the lifeblood of the company, were not going to be renewed. We scrambled in our department, developing models to repair the finances, to stay alive. We analyzed how we could cut expenses, close divisions, lay off people, and buy back our bonds, which quickly went from high-grade to junk status.

I learned that Intellogic Trace had no contingency plan and a mindset that was not future-oriented, and

I left and moved to Denver before the company dissolved. I saw, firsthand, how an established business can evaporate and become worthless.

The point here is that a company must be future-oriented and have contingency plans for adapting to rapid change, and the more capable the management team and the business is of adaptability, the better off an investment can turn out to be for you.

Desirability

Companies that focus their attention on understanding their customers and doing things to provide more value to them have high desirability. They create new products and services that help customers succeed. Highly desirable businesses strive to be unique when designing what they deliver to customers and spend less time trying to copy what competitors do. They anticipate customer needs, listen intently, and constantly develop new capabilities that customers want. They seek to shape the future rather than be a slave to the past way of doing things.

Profitability

Companies can be great investments if they can become more and more profitable over time. A company's ability to raise prices to match or exceed inflation is often a good sign. Companies that do not require a large amount of capital to invest as they grow also increase profitability. These companies tend to be scalable because they can grow without large new hirings or the purchase of expensive equipment. The prospects for higher profits are even better if a company has intellectual capital, which gives them know-how and processes or a legal advantage that other competitors cannot easily match. They must be able to attract new customers without spending a lot of money. You want to avoid companies that will struggle to gain profits because all the money goes out the door trying to get new customers.

These are some of the most important elements to look for when assessing an investment for profitability. All of these factors can increase profits over time and help a company beat the competition.

There are basically four types of stocks in this environment. It is not always clear where each company fits, but this general framework can help determine what to own and what to avoid. Here are the four main four categories:

- old economy companies that are successfully reinventing their business model for the future
- old economy companies that are troubled and cannot adapt to the new future
- new economy companies with highly desirable new products or services that are breaking into profitability

- new economy companies with new products or services that are struggling to reach profitability

This method isolates opportunities for you to win regardless of the craziness that may be going on around you.

ADP Criteria

Focus Your Capital in Companies with a High ADP Rank

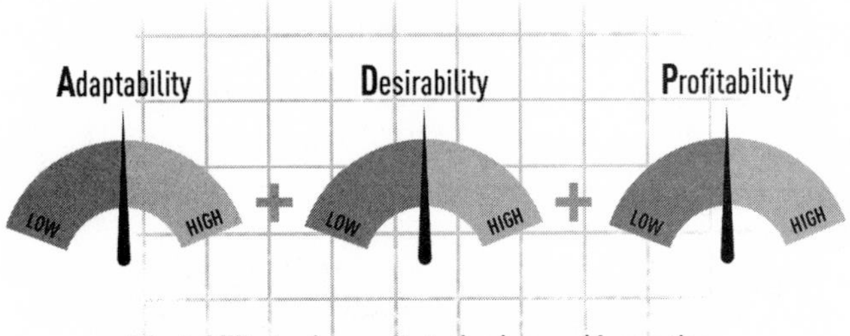

Adaptability to changes in technology and innovation
Desirability of product or service now and in the future
Profitability of the business now and in the future

The companies that do not meet the ADP Criteria are eliminated from consideration for investments in this framework. Companies that are successfully reinventing themselves to profit from the future should remain in your portfolio.

The Mattress and the Drawer Solution

It can be easy to feel paralyzed about the stock market. I recently got off the phone with a potential new investor, with a multimillion-dollar portfolio, who told me flat out, "I don't know what to do because I see all these risks around me. I just want to stick all of my money in a drawer." Many have responded to similar fears by hiding their wealth under a mattress.

But you can't really do that. Why? Because taxes and inflation will eat you alive. If inflation starts to rise as governments continue to print money repeatedly, your money is worth less, and it loses value just sitting there. The "mattress strategy" is especially bad if you need a sustainable income stream for the long term, draining your money even faster at whatever rate necessary to provide support. Additionally, you may live longer than you think. Today, a sixty-year-old will probably live twenty to thirty years while taking income. You must ensure your money will last.

Bonds Are Not Safe in the Long Run

We will have different economic cycles and conditions that will affect your returns. As of this writing, interest rates are near zero. After taxes and inflation, you have negative returns in the so-called "safe" investment in Treasury notes issued by the United States government. How safe are bonds really over the long term? You're not likely to get ahead with a portfolio filled only with fixed-income investments.

Warm and Fuzzy Means Low Returns

Many people like to invest in a portfolio of "warm and fuzzy" stocks; that is, a portfolio filled with familiar household names that seem to have a stable business. These stocks seem safe, and you may have a sense of security owning them. Some of these companies may be great investments. But many of them will wind up being part of the "old economy" because they are unable to adapt to the future or are highly regulated.

Unfortunately, buying and holding a portfolio filled with warm and fuzzy stocks may give you a false sense of hope. Warm and fuzzy companies that are unable to adapt can go out of business during periods of rapid change. Others can fall dramatically and not recover in value for over a decade. Some blue-chip companies are from the past, they're not part of the future, and they may not be able to adapt well. It is better to evaluate each company based on the ADP Criteria outlined earlier in this chapter. You may have a little more turnover in your portfolio, because you may need to sell companies that do not meet your criteria, but it will keep you from holding clunkers too long.

Innovation Economy

Real money can be made in the younger, more dynamic companies you've probably never even heard of. If you don't invest a portion of your money in fast-growing young companies, then you are missing out on great opportunities. It will be hard for you to get reasonably good returns without owning stocks in the innovation economy.

Narrative versus Numbers

Have you ever turned on the financial news and listened to an analyst or portfolio manager tell you a story about a company that is poised for a big move up? Maybe the company is in an exciting area that could explode in the future. Stories are compelling to us humans because our brains are wired to follow and remember stories. Stories motivate us. I have no problem investing in a good story stock, but it must be backed by numbers.

So, when you hear an elaborate story and gravitate toward the idea of investing in the stock—STOP!

Stop, and ask:

- Does the company have real revenue growth?
- Do they have a business model that can break into profitability soon, or are they already profitable?
- Is the balance sheet flush with cash and little debt so they can weather a storm?
- Who are their competitors?

- Can the competition squash this company's plans quickly and easily?

- Is the stock price trending higher, showing that the market is recognizing the company's future?

A story stock without strong financial numbers is like peanut butter without jelly. Without numbers to back up the story, you might get peanut butter stuck on the roof of your mouth.

Recipe for Stock Selection

Investing successfully is like great cooking. It requires a recipe (a formula) that leads to tasty food in a consistent way. Your stock recipe is simply a checklist to help you stay on track. If you follow the recipe, you will lean the odds in your favor to pick winners. Not every stock will be a winner, but if you combine the recipe with risk management and portfolio construction protocols, then you will have a long-term winning recipe.

I want to share a formula I developed for trading and investing in stocks. This formula gives you the tools to find the right stocks, where to focus your capital, and how to invest profitably. It is a further refinement of the stocks that meet the ADP Criteria.

You only make money when the market RECOGNIZES the value of your holdings and pushes them higher in price.

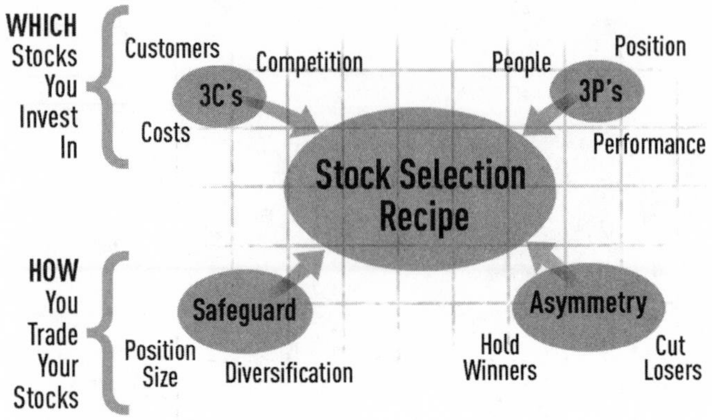

Stock Selection = 3P+3C+SA

You Can Trade Stocks Profitably

If you are like most people, you want to grow your money in stocks, but you're worried about losing money. I developed this formula and have been successfully managing millions of dollars for clients and myself. Over time, this philosophy has helped me avoid stocks that are too risky, and increase the probability that my stock investments will make money. This strategy, combined with smart diversification, can help you improve your growth and protect your money.

Here is the formula:

3 Cs + 3 Ps + SA

The 3 Cs and the 3 Ps give you the ammunition to find *what* stocks to focus on for investment. The "SA" part of the formula explains *how* to trade the stocks.

Let's start with the 3 Cs. The first "C" stands for *customers*. Who are their customers? Are their customers stable? Are customers growing and doing well? Are they price-sensitive, or are they willing to pay higher prices? Customers are the lifeblood of the business. That is the best starting point when selecting stocks. You are looking for customers that are growing in number and willing to pay higher prices. It's better if they are repeat customers.

The second "C" stands for *competitive advantage*. Does the company have a product or service that is truly better or more desirable than the competition? Is their business a game-changer or in a new product category? The competitive advantage is important because it will determine if customers buy this company's products over the competition now and in the future.

The third "C" stands for *costs*. What is the cost of doing business for this company? Are their profit margins high, medium, or low? Are the costs likely to increase or decrease? Can this company face radically higher costs for some reason? Are the costs volatile and subject to sudden and large changes up or down? The costs are important because this affects the chance the company can withstand a sudden loss.

3 Ps

Now let us go over the 3 Ps. The first "P" stands for *people*. Who are the key people on the management team? Do they have a track record of doing a good job? Do they make sound decisions with capital, or do they spend it unwisely?

The second "P" stands for *position*. What is the company's financial position? Do they have a lot of cash on the balance sheet, or do they have a little cash? You obviously want more cash on the balance sheet to protect your investment. Do they have a high amount of debt or a low amount? Although this is not an exhaustive list of the financial position, the two most important factors are the cash position and the debt amounts.

The last "P" stands for *performance*. Is the stock being recognized in the marketplace for doing well? You should see the stock outperforming the market and trending higher.

I have a simple acronym used to analyze the performance of a stock. The acronym is *TORQ*. It stands for Trend, Overbought/Oversold, Relative Strength, and Quality Patterns. The TORQ analysis helps you determine if the stock price is acting healthy with good supply-and-demand characteristics.

Here are the basic questions to ask:

- Is the stock price trending higher?
- Is the stock price overextended or still buyable now?

- Is the stock price outperforming or lagging the overall stock market?

- Is the psychology positive based on the pattern of supply and demand?

Now, that covers the "*what* should I buy?" portion of the formula. The stocks that pass the ADP Criteria and the 3 Cs and 3 Ps are worthy of investment. Now let's discuss the "*how* do I trade the stock?" portion of the formula.

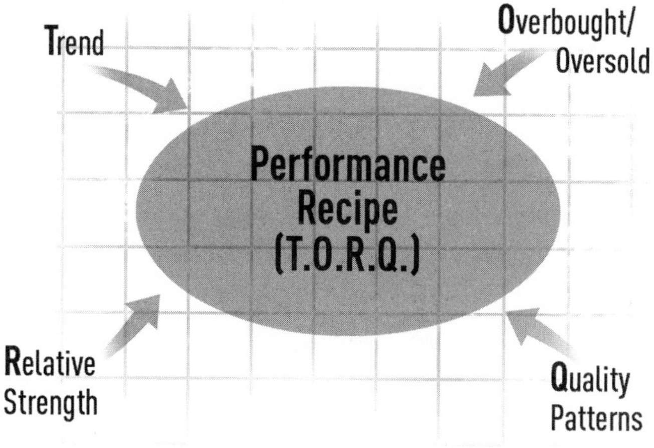

Performance=T.O.R.Q.

How to Trade Your Stocks

In the last part of the stock selection formula, the "S" stands for *safeguard*. Rule number one is to safeguard through position sizing and predefining your risk.

You must pre-determine how much you're going to risk *before* you invest or trade a stock. This amount will help you determine how much of your capital to put into each stock. You must make sure that you give your stocks enough room to hold them through normal volatility. You also need to have a level for which, no matter what your view of the fundamentals, you will cut your losses short if the stock moves against you. No matter how great your fundamental analysis is, you must cut your losses to mathematically allow your profits to outweigh your losses. Maybe the markets were not right; maybe the government is doing something to hurt your investment.

Next, the "A" stands for *asymmetric*. That is just a fancy word for finding opportunities that have limited downside and a very large upside potential. You want to cut your losses short and let your profits run. This approach will help you achieve an asymmetric payoff, where the upside is very big relative to how much you're risking.

So that's the formula. If you follow these factors, you are likely to increase your profits and avoid big losses.

Correcting your mistakes is more important than perfect timing.

Seven Steps to Map Your Future 2

In preparing for battle I have always found that plans are useless, but planning is indispensable.

—Dwight D. Eisenhower

I've discovered that a multistep planning process is the most effective way to deliver increased wealth and happiness. It is a process to clarify your goals and develop a doable action plan to achieve them. Indeed, it's a well-thought-out framework to make smart financial choices. This section will discuss the step-by-step financial planning process that I recommend.

This procedure has been developed over years of practical experience and is designed to work for you regardless of your circumstances. Don't be fooled by its simplicity. There is *power* in minimalism.

Planning will focus your attention on the long-term picture encompassing a holistic view of your life, not only your money.

You may be wondering why it's necessary to talk about financial planning rather than jumping right to investment strategies. It's easy to make a decision today based on a short-term concern, but in the process, you may compromise your long-term goals. If you get too far off track because of short-term worries, it's harder to regain your footing to reach your final destination. Too many detours can be destructive and can lead to time lost and inefficient actions. Preparation will help you avoid these mistakes.

Avoid Making Mistakes

One of the most common blunders is paying taxes that arise from unnecessary transactions or improperly structured accounts. It's frustrating when you realize after the fact that you could have avoided paying taxes. If you follow the process I am about to show you, paying too much in taxes is less likely to happen. Another mistake due to poor planning is taking on too much risk. Proper planning will predefine your risk and provide a strategy that you can live with. Improper risk management almost always leads to permanent losses. Poor investment choices also come from improper planning. This planning process will equip you with clear guidelines that can keep you headed in the right direction.

Because your situation is unique, your plan should be designed around your present circumstances and preferences. Suitable planning should not be cookie-cutter. One of the biggest problems that I see in the marketplace today is that a lot of planning services are not really providing true customization. They're actually providing advice based exclusively on computer formulas or algorithms. But those algorithms can't know your family. They can't know how you feel about risk. They can't know your unique tax situation or your distinctive time horizon.

I believe that sophisticated algorithms and the latest technology *should* be used as a tool to help in the process, but nothing replaces the judgment of a trained human being who knows how to use the tools appropriately.

A good plan must answer the following major questions:

- What is my financial picture today?
- What is my ideal future?
- Are there obstacles I need to overcome?
- What specific actions can I take to reach my goals?

Making Smart Financial Choices

You can't make smart financial choices unless you quantify your goals. You must aim for a clear target by defining dollar amounts and timelines. This will help you decide on the appropriate actions you will need to take. With this plan, you will understand the amount of money each goal can cost and what that means in today's dollars. Knowing those *magic numbers* will allow you to focus on important decisions that maximize your net worth and income.

Consequently, you'll gain confidence that you are doing the right thing for your future.

Establish Checkpoints to Keep on Track

If your financial route is laid out ahead of time, you will recognize if you're off track. Along your path in life, you can compare your actual wealth with your targets. Through regular reviews you can correct your course. It may be necessary to review your situation regularly, especially if the economy or your personal situation changes enough to warrant an update to your portfolio.

You are a human
being, not a number.

A computer cannot
know your family,
your goals, or all
your circumstances.

You are a unique
person that requires
a tailored solution
for your future.

Seven-Step Process for Planning

I recommend a seven-step planning process to guide your investing. It's important to do the steps in sequence so you get the best results. Otherwise, you will find yourself spending more time to get them done. Reduce the hassle and do them in order.

Step One:
Identify and Prioritize Objectives

The first step is to create an ideal vision for your future and to identify your important goals. I've found that there are five types of questions we can ask ourselves to identify our real goals.

They are questions of

- purpose and values;
- opportunities and threats;
- visualizing your future;
- goal transformation; and
- the wider impact of your goals.

Being rich is empty without a purpose in life. Take time to reflect on your own personal values and what they mean to you; discuss them with your partner and your advisors. Huge rewards can be reaped from this alone because the hardest part of planning is getting clear on what you want. These two questions will address your long-term values:

- What is the single focus and activity that would keep you absolutely fascinated and motivated for the rest of your life?
- What is important about money to you? Specify why it is important.

OPPORTUNITIES AND THREATS

Sometimes short-term obstacles can stifle your progress toward your long-term goals. Overcoming them is the key to breaking through to the next level. Here are some questions to identify your short-term obstacles:

- If you were to look at your life three years from today, what must happen both personally and professionally during that period for you to feel happy with your progress?
- What are the three biggest dangers to achieving your goals?

- What are the biggest opportunities you must focus on and capture now?

- What are the three biggest strengths you must reinforce and maximize?

VISUALIZING YOUR FUTURE

To realize your ideal future, you have to make changes in yourself. Part of your past is important for your future, and other parts are irrelevant and should be discarded. *You* get to choose what comes along for the ride in your future. The past does not equal the future.

Answer these three questions to see what changes in yourself may be necessary and what baggage must be discarded:

- What future do you want and choose for yourself?

- What part of your past must be part of your future and come along for the ride?

- What do you want to utilize in the present to get the best possible outcome?

Now it's time to put your values and obstacles together and seek solutions. This requires you to visualize your future and define your desired results, the obstacles in the way, and how you will overcome them.

Your decisions about finances must support your relationships and the activities that you enjoy.

Money alone will not make you happy.

The following questions can help you transform your goals into actions:

- What is your vision for a bigger, better future? (Picture it in your mind with all your senses.)
- What is your desired result? (How would it look if you could not fail?)
- What is the best possible outcome?
- What is your measure for success?
- How will you know you've achieved the goal?
- What obstacles could make it impossible to achieve your goal or could limit it? (Think of everything that could prevent your goal from being achieved. Are there any strategies you can think of that can overcome your obstacles?)
- Are there any people or resources you need to delegate to or get expertise from?

You need to check to see if you really want the goals you set. The pain associated with not achieving your goals must be significant. You need the *why* for your goals.

Answer these questions to discover if your goals are really meaningful to you. If they aren't, perhaps they should be revised:

- What would happen if you did not achieve your goal?
- If you did not achieve your goal, what effect would it have on you and the people who are important to you?
- Could failing to achieve your goal lead to any problems, difficulties, or dissatisfaction?
- Why is it important to solve the challenges to achieve your goals? (Is this goal really worthwhile?)
- Is there another way to realize your goals that can help you?
- Should any of your goals be modified or eliminated?

Now that you are clear about what your goals are, it's time to prioritize them. I call this process goal grading. Goal grading has three steps.

Step One: Score by Viewpoint

The first step is to assess each goal from five different viewpoints—urgency, relationships, passions, health, and your other values like community, spirituality, and effects on society. For each goal, ask yourself how the goal affects you from each viewpoint. How urgent is it? How does it reflect my relationships? Is it aligned with my passions, health, spiritual pursuits, and my beliefs about society or my community? Assign a number from one to five for each viewpoint for each goal.

For example, let's say your first goal is to retire at age fifty-five. Rate this goal at five for urgency if you think this is an urgent goal. Rate it at one if it is not urgent. Do the same for each viewpoint.

Step Two: Total Goal Score

The second step is to add up the viewpoint scores for each goal to get the total score for each goal. This will be the overall score for that particular goal.

The last step is to compare the overall score for each goal and rank them. The goal with the highest score is the most important for your financial plan.

Here are some useful questions for each viewpoint to spur your thoughts and to get clear about what is important:

- *Urgency*—How urgent is the goal? Does any goal need to be reached sooner rather than later? (one = not urgent, five = urgent)

- *People*—How does this goal affect the people who are important to me? Is the impact good or bad for my family, friends, and colleagues? (one = bad for relationships, five = good for relationships)

- *Passions*—Does this goal move me toward my passions in life? (one = away from my passions, five = toward my passions)

- *Health*—How does this goal affect my health and happiness? (one = bad for health, five = good for health)

- *Other Values*—Does the goal help me actualize my higher purpose? Does this goal move me toward the societal or community goals that I would like to achieve during my lifetime? (one = not aligned with my values, five = highly aligned with my values)

Goal Grading

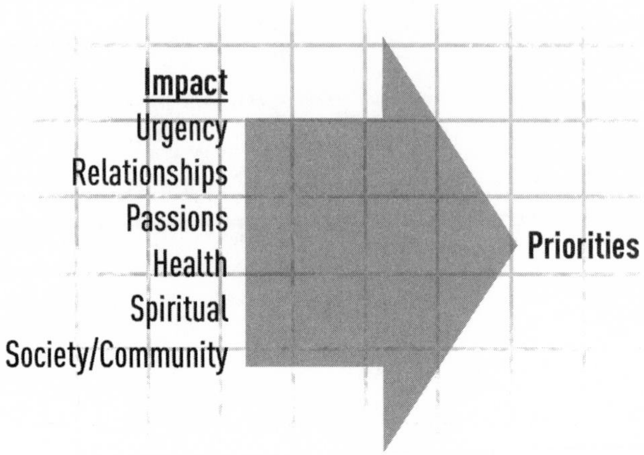

After doing this, you should know which goals should take precedence over the others. Your priorities will then be used when it comes time to determine how to allocate your investments and future savings.

Step Two: Get Organized and Gather Data

Congratulations, you now have clear goals and your priorities in place. Now it's time to get organized so you can see your financial picture clearly. You will need to gather all important documents related to your finances (see the Document Checklist in the Appendix).

Stack and arrange your documents into the following categories:

1. assets—anything you own
2. liabilities—money you owe
3. income—all income sources like salaries, rental income, pensions, etc.
4. expenses—your mandatory and discretionary expenses
5. other—insurance policies, benefits, tax returns, etc.

Next, your data will be entered into a sophisticated financial planning software program to be manipulated in many different reports. Having all of your financial data in one spot will help you discover the overall allocation of your assets and how your debt is structured. It may reveal actions you can take to lower expenses and taxes while increasing savings. After you see your full financial picture, you may want to reassess what is important to you and reshuffle your priorities.

It is best to assess your risk tolerance at this point. This includes gaining a clear understanding of how you feel about risk and in what manner this will fit your situation. This involves a risk tolerance questionnaire. This book does not include a risk tolerance questionnaire, but note that this is part of the Document Checklist in the Appendix. I discuss the subject of risk tolerance in more depth in Chapter 4, "Protect Your Money."

I recommend using secure technology to scan and place this information in a location that you can access no matter where you happen to be. If you travel, this digital collection can be very handy. It's also helpful for collaborating with advisors like your CPA, financial planner, and attorney. A data-aggregation platform can provide this technology service. The best platforms are available online through financial advisory firms, but some retail products are also available.

WHAT TO LOOK FOR IN FINANCIAL PLANNING SOFTWARE

When using financial planning software, there are some important capabilities to look out for. Here are the important capabilities that the software should be able to do for you:

First, the software should have a comprehensive fact-finding database that can help you keep track of your financial priorities, goals, net worth, income, and expenses. It should be able to estimate your taxes based on the current tax rules and be flexible enough to make changes to your assumptions now and in the future. The software should keep track of all your savings and contributions to retirement accounts for yourself and your employer. It should provide a detailed analysis of your investment asset allocation and a detailed analysis of any insurance and protection.

Second, the financial planning software must be able to make extensive calculations that are integrated across your entire financial situation, including all of your assets, liabilities, income, and expenses. The software should forecast your net worth, using two different methods: goals-based and cash-flow-based. Goals-based forecasts isolate a goal and calculate without detailed cash flows. The cash-flow method makes detailed year-by-year calculations to forecast your results. At times, both methods may be needed, depending on your situation.

Third, the engine should be able to create and compare scenarios based on a "what-if" analysis. For example, what happens if I sell my home, retire early, or sell stock? It should be able to solve different ways to reach your goals, such as retirement, funding your children's education, or leaving an inheritance. It should have a Monte Carlo simulation capability that will allow you to stress test your portfolio when the economy is good or bad. It should also handle the type of assets that you own, such as stock options from work, restricted stock units, real estate, businesses, trusts, and other complex situations that apply to you.

Fourth, a good financial planning software program will provide a wide variety of reports. The program should have clear reports, such as cash-flow forecasts, financial projections, worksheets, and schedules. These reports can help you track your progress and adjust over time.

Fifth, the software should have a vault to securely store your documents in a central location. A major problem people have is that they can't find information quickly. If you have a great vault, you can swiftly find your documents when you need them. This comes in handy when your CPA, attorney, or insurance agent is requesting information.

Lastly, your financial planning software should have an excellent data aggregation capability. Data aggregation is a technology that links all of your accounts to your financial planning software. This will allow the software to automatically update the values of your accounts from data provided by your banks, investment firms, retirement accounts at work, credit cards, and mortgages. You will have the most recent information at your fingertips, and you will save time because less manual data entry is required.

The best software programs have changed many times over the years. As of this writing, the highest-rated financial planning software programs that are used by top financial advisors include eMoney, MoneyGuide Pro, Naviplan, and MoneyTree.

GARBAGE IN, GARBAGE OUT

A word of caution about financial planning software: the software is only as good as the knowledge of the user. If the wrong information is input, the answers for solving problems will be wrong. Because the best financial planning software is performing complex calculations, and the financial planning field is intricate, the user must know what they are doing. If the user does not completely understand how the calculations are made and where data is being pulled from, the forecasts may be wrong. The user must know how to validate the calculations prior to using them for decision-making. This goes for all financial analysis—garbage in leads to garbage out.

The proper use of financial planning tools takes education and skill. For many people, it takes years for them to be proficient at using powerful financial planning software. Our experience at my firm is that it usually takes a credentialed and financially-educated person two years before they are fully functional and able to independently create accurate financial plans. This is for a credentialled individual with a CPA, CFP, or CFA designation prior to using the software. This gives them the educational background necessary to be able to verify the data.

With that said, there are software programs for individuals to do their own financial plans. But I caution you about using them. It reminds me of people who use TurboTax to do their taxes. If you have a very simple situation, you may be able to use TurboTax to do your taxes. But once your situation gets a little more complicated, it becomes difficult to do your taxes accurately. To avoid costly errors, you probably will be better off hiring an experienced certified public accountant. This provides the peace of mind that your taxes were done correctly. The same principle applies to the financial planning field. The more complex your situation, the more advantageous it is for you to hire a credentialed and experienced financial advisory firm to navigate the financial planning tools for you.

Step Three: Analyze Your Situation

Once you've got the data organized, it can be analyzed to compare where you are today to where you want to be in the future. The financial planning software comes in handy to perform two tasks: goal-based planning and cash-flow forecasting.

Goal-based planning helps you estimate the cost of your goals and lays out the timeline for investing and withdrawing money. It can also calculate how much money you will need to accumulate, then tell you how much to invest at various rates of return. This is called a *needs analysis*.

On the other hand, *cash-flow forecasting* is a powerful model capable of calculating the details of your cash flows. The intricate account rules for taxes, estate planning, and investment details are forecasted using this module.

Combining both the goal-based planning and cash-flow forecasting models will provide the number-crunching power needed to analyze your finances under various economic conditions.

Although there are many free online calculators, they are usually incomplete. To get the full power needed, I recommend working with a competent planner with access to top-notch planning software. It is important to get accurate answers to solve financial challenges.

Step Four: Develop Realistic Solutions by Evaluating Alternatives

By now you and your advisors have analyzed the data. Now it's time to develop a realistic solution for generating income for the rest of your life. Estimating how much money you will need to provide for your lifestyle requires crunching the numbers of various scenarios. The ultimate goal of this step is to find your target level of wealth and how you are going to get it.

Let's call the sum of money you will need to be financially independent your magic number. This number is discovered by projecting your cash flows into the future and then discounting them back to the day that you are financially independent. I like to call this day your financial independence day. From there, it is a simple task of finding out the amount of savings needed each month, quarter, or year to reach the goal, given a range of returns. The returns used are based on your risk profile and the long-run expected returns in various asset classes.

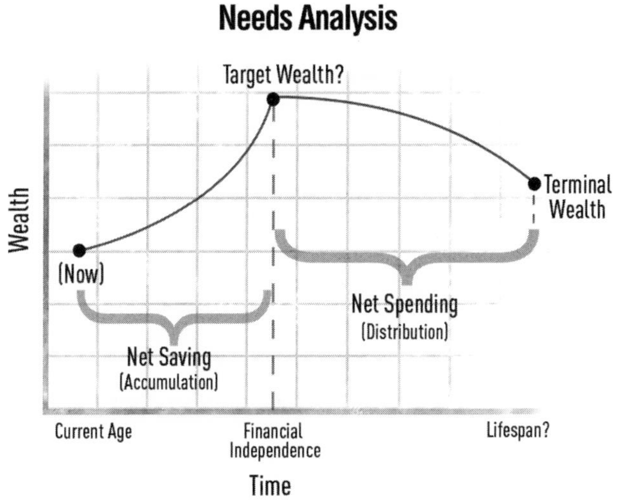

Developing Realistic Solutions

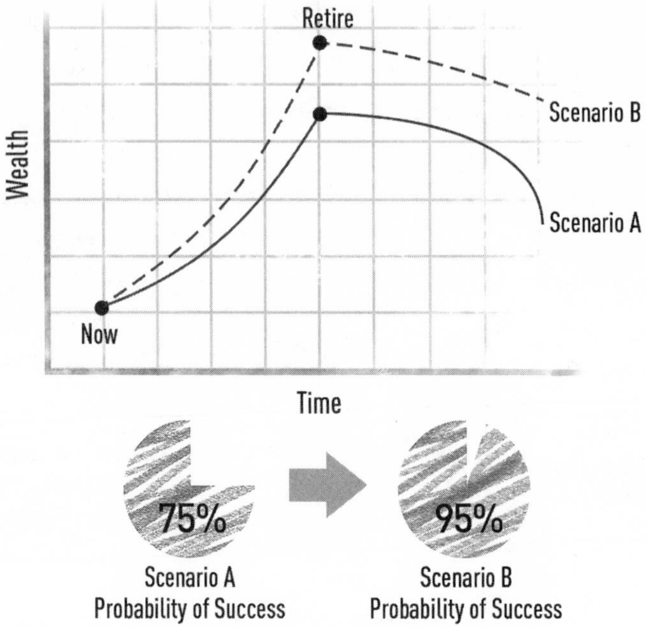

One of the best ways to solve any financial challenge is to create and evaluate actionable alternatives and to evaluate the merit of each scenario.

Organize, simplify, and multiply your wealth.

In the end, you should be able to choose the option that best meets your goals. At first, your ultimate plan may be hidden, but this brainstorming process usually provides a solution. Working with an advisor at this stage can be helpful because she will probably have much more experience solving these challenges and will offer ways to shorten the time necessary to get good answers.

Before you decide on your alternative, it's important to discuss any differences you have with your spouse or significant other. Even though it's unpleasant, it's a good idea to spend some time thinking about what can go wrong. If you are married, you and your spouse may have different feelings about risk. Discussing and debating your views will often reveal concerns that could cause conflict. Deliberating this ahead of time will help you avoid future problems. If you are single, it's best to consult with the most important people in your life. Together you can develop a workable plan that is less likely to go astray down the road.

Step Five: Develop Your Investment Policy

At this point, you should be armed with a clear vision about your goals and a solution to achieve them. Now it's time to document your investment plan so you can have a source to refer to. This becomes important as time moves forward because your investment policy statement (IPS) will provide a framework for making decisions. Undoubtedly, you will have constraints that will affect how your investments will be managed. Written guidelines will help you and your advisors stick with the plan. Savvy institutions and high-net-worth individuals have been using IPS documents for years for one simple reason: they work.

Here are the basic elements of an IPS:

- description of your circumstances
- statement of goals and constraints
- investment strategies and styles to be used
- schedule for reviewing performance
- description of performance benchmarks
- any special circumstances and preferences

Both your head and your heart must agree with your decisions.

Your IPS should state a range of expected returns based on a realistic estimate derived from both historical data and forward-looking analysis. Keep in mind that your risk tolerance should be congruent with your return requirement. It is not appropriate to expect your portfolio to produce high returns while maintaining a low-risk profile because the two do not go hand in hand. Obviously, higher returns involve higher risks and vice versa.

How long you expect to be adding money to your accounts and when you will need to spend from them both play a crucial role in constructing your portfolio. A good explanation of the timing of cash flows will be needed so that your portfolio can be invested to maximize returns and minimize risk in your time horizon. Legal limitations that affect your situation should be stated as well. Once the IPS is done, it's time to implement your plan.

Step Six: Implement Your Plan

Now that the groundwork is laid, you can take action to rebalance your accounts. In the event that your investments need to be adjusted, look for the most efficient way to transition your accounts to the new target allocation. Be sure to minimize unnecessary transaction costs and taxes that can hurt results. Usually, it's a good idea to consolidate your accounts because it simplifies administrative tasks in the future.

Any estate-planning issues should be resolved, ensuring that the account titles are correct and the beneficiaries match your will or trust. Insurance policies, benefit plans, annuities, and retirement accounts should also be adjusted as necessary. You want to double-check that interested parties, such as family and charities, are not adversely affected by your actions. After your investments are moved and settled, a review should be done to confirm all is in order.

Step Seven: Monitor Your Progress

The next step is to monitor and review your progress on a regular basis. There are four things to do during a review:

1. Review your objectives to make sure they have not changed.

2. Verify that you are on pace to reach your goals.

3. Examine your existing holdings compared to an appropriate benchmark.

4. Make adjustments for changes in your circumstances and/or the markets.

USING TECHNOLOGY FOR REVIEWS

Reviewing a portfolio is more enjoyable with the help of efficient technology. All of your important financial reports should be in a single portal that allows you to quickly access information about your assets, liabilities, income, and expenses. The system should combine your total investments, such as your 401(k), brokerage, and bank accounts, even if they're located at different financial institutions.

Your real-estate and business assets should also be included in this accounting so you can see your big picture. Important documents, such as insurance policies, wills, trusts, Social Security, and employee benefits, should also be stored in a private electronic vault.

This comes in handy when you are traveling or need to get information quickly. This type of technology is called *account aggregation*. Over the years, well over 600,000 financial institutions have linked their data to account-aggregation portals. I highly recommend using this technology; it will make your life easier.

TACTICAL SHIFTS AND REBALANCING

As the economy changes, some investments become more attractive than others. Investments that were once values become overpriced and should be sold. Of course, the opposite can be true. It may be better to invest in new, promising opportunities. Tactical shifts in the portfolio are designed to adjust your portfolio for these dynamics.

A different trading tool is *rebalancing*. The value of your investments can deviate substantially from your target percentages. If the variance is too large, it is beneficial for your portfolio to be rebalanced.

To illustrate a simple example, let's say your stocks have risen in value over the past year while your bonds were stable. As a result of these market movements, you have a bigger percentage of your assets in stocks and a lower percentage in bonds. Because your stocks grew considerably more than your bonds, your risk is now outside of your comfort zone. When this happens, sell a portion of your stocks and buy bonds with the proceeds. After this is completed, your portfolio will be back in line with your tolerance for risk.

I recommend establishing a comfort zone that defines how much you will allow your risk to vary from your target. This is known as a *drift tolerance parameter*. Drift parameters can be applied to individual investments as well as your overall portfolio.

The amount that should be allowed to drift is related to your target weight and volatility of each investment. Highly-volatile investments can easily throw your portfolio out of your comfort zone, whereas more stable assets will not. Similarly, investments that have a large percentage of money allocated to them have a higher propensity to cause your portfolio to drift. This occurs because a small percentage change in the value of a large allocation could result in a large change in the risk of the portfolio.

It's a good idea to rebalance only after considering transaction costs and taxes. Rebalancing should not be done too frequently because it will generate short-term capital gains and transaction costs that will lower your returns. It should only be done when the benefits outweigh the costs.

Another reason to fine-tune your investment strategy is because your personal circumstances have changed.

Substantial life events will inevitably alter your goals. Maybe you've inherited some money or your income has risen.

Everyone's priorities evolve over time, which leads you to change your goals too. It is not uncommon for family dynamics or other relationships to alter your financial needs. When this happens to you, be sure to adjust your finances.

Follow these steps and you will be clear on your values and goals. You and your spouse will agree on the direction for your future. Your important documents will be organized so you can see where you stand at a glance. Your portfolio will be managed so you can stick with it for the long term. You'll gain peace of mind knowing that you have guidelines for handling your assets when markets are volatile. You're going to have clear strategies and actions to reach your goals. Last, but not least, you will have a solid method to monitor your progress and make adjustments along your journey.

STEPS	TASKS
Step 1 Identify & Prioritize Goals	• Core Vision • Goal Grading • Risk Preference
Step 2 Gather & Organize Data	• Document Check List • Input Data
Step 3 Analyze Current Situation	• Strengths • Opportunities • Threats
Step 4 Develop Realistic Solutions	• Base Case • Stress-Test Scenarios • Decide on Action Plan
Step 5 Investment Policy	• Risk/Return • Liquidity and Income • Constraints
Step 6 Implement	• Account Administration • Asset Location and Trading
Step 7 Monitor Progress	• Review Goals • Verify Allocations • Make Adjustments

3 Throw Away the Dartboard

Not only do investors go wrong, they go wrong in a systematic and predictable manner.

So predictable, in fact, that consistent investment strategies can be built on their mistakes.

—David Dreman

In my view, *the* most effective way to invest is to follow the evidence. Evidence-based investing uses methods to analyze facts to make investment decisions. Strategies are tested to verify their ability to add value in the investment process. We, as investors, need a sound foundation for making investment decisions that are not clouded by human flaws and emotions. It's amazing how often people invest based on tips, news, or opinions rather than sound factual research. What we really want to do is *think like a doctor or a scientist.*

Investors should think like a doctor or a scientist, not a gambler. Invest your money, backed by data and logic, not gut feelings or emotions. It takes discipline to safeguard your money.

Think Like a Scientist

A good investment manager should think like a doctor who has a scientific mindset. In the medical industry, statistical methods and logic are used to determine if a drug or surgical technique is viable. It should be no different for investing. For example, if a new surgical technique or drug is being considered to cure cancer, scientists will rigorously look at its effectiveness. They will sample data, calculate statistics, and determine probabilities to see if the technique or medicine gets better results than random chance or a placebo test. They will determine if it's going to do any harm to patients. Scientists will also determine how effectively the treatment works across many different types of patients.

You are neither right nor wrong because people agree with you.

—Benjamin Graham

Likewise, asset managers should conduct rigorous research and ask questions, such as these:

- If I had used this strategy over time, what would the results have been?
- What were the returns and risks compared to passive indexes?

- Are the returns satisfactory after taxes, transaction costs, and impact costs?

- How did the strategy perform when markets were volatile, quiet, and upward and downward trending?

- Is the tactic robust enough to work under extreme market conditions?

- What are the underlying drivers of returns, and does it make logical sense that these assumptions will be true in the future?

- What is the chance that this strategy will perform better than randomly throwing a dart?

Your Millionaire Mind

People don't want to admit their faults, but only good investors recognize them as soon as possible. It is not natural for most of us to seek our own faults. It requires a complete mindset shift.

Scientific evidence proves that we tend to make systematic mistakes regardless of our intellect.

Professors and scientists in academia have developed an entire field called behavioral finance. They have found human judgment to be seriously flawed when it comes to investing. Evidence-based strategies help you become aware of these mistakes so you can make more rational choices.

Here are a few common flaws to avoid.

Herding Behavior

Herding behavior is the tendency for individuals to mimic the actions of other people, whether those actions are rational or not. Individually, most people will not necessarily make irrational choices, but when we are a part of a large group, we tend to follow the herd. We all want to think we are rational beings, but that's not supported by facts. We need to think independently.

Overconfidence

This feeling leads us to trade too often or invest too heavily in a particular asset. We're self-assured of our superiority. Not everyone can be an above-average investor, yet we all tend to think we are! This can lead people to trust their gut rather than do the homework. Believe it or not, many times a gut feeling is not a good source for decision-making.

This is another phenomenon that leads investors into poor decision-making. Our brains are hardwired to hold losers too long and sell winners too soon. In 1979, Daniel Kahneman and Amos Tversky developed the prospect theory when their research found that people do not value gains the same as losses.[1] The evidence suggests that we want to hold our losers to avoid regret and circumvent the pain of admitting a mistake.

This behavior leads to larger losses while investors wait on the hope of a rebound in their losers. On the other hand, it is easy for us take a quick gain because it makes us feel better. This is the exact opposite behavior needed to generate strong returns. Instead, we need to cut our losers short and let our winners run to increase our profits.

This is known as *trend following*.

Overreaction

Overreaction describes the tendency for people to overreact to new information. How many times are we swayed by the financial news or some other media? In many cases, this leads investors to buy or sell immediately without knowing the facts or estimating the consequences. Inevitably, prices will overshoot up or down. This "important" news means nothing to the value of assets a year or two later. Because investors overreact to news, securities can be mispriced, whether undervalued or overvalued. A savvy investor can identify this opportunity and buy when others sell impulsively on negative news. The inverse is also true. A security can be overvalued as investors buy in a knee-jerk reaction to positive news. If you are doing your homework, you can profit from other investors' overreaction to prices by buying during panics and selling during euphoria.

Recency

We are prone to place more importance on recent information than on older data. This is a problem because something that happened today is not necessarily more important than if it happened last week. New information is so fresh in our minds that we don't see the full picture. As we will discuss, an evidence-based approach helps to reduce this error in judgment.

Eliminate Hidden, Overlapping Investments

The only free lunch on Wall Street is diversification. It sounds so simple. How hard can it be? Just don't put all your eggs in one basket, right? Well, not exactly. It can be tricky because your holdings don't always play by the rules of diversification. If you own mutual or exchange-traded funds (ETFs), there could be overlapping securities within them. It's not easy to see your common risks among holdings. To make matters more complicated, individual stocks tend to move down in price when volatility increases, so we lose diversification at the exact moment we need it the most.

Overlapping Investments = Less Diversification

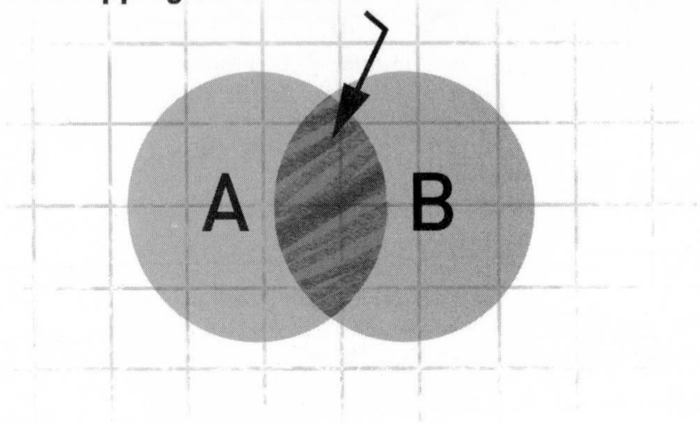

Are You Really Diversified?

We all know that wealth is destroyed during bear markets.

During these periods, virtually all stocks move down at the same time while volatility rises. This happens in both the U.S. and international markets; it doesn't matter if you diversify globally. So just when you want more diversification, you get less of it. To learn more about this problem, read Chapter 13, "Converging Correlation and Market Shocks," my contribution to the book *The Handbook of Risk* (Wiley, 2003).[2]

So, what should investors do to improve diversification? The usual advice is to diversify across asset classes, geography, market capitalization, and investment styles. Although this is sound advice, if it is applied just to buying *long-only* investing, your portfolio is still subject to problems with converging correlation. But what about when markets are stressed and many investments are going down at the same time? This is when *non-correlated absolute-return investments* come in handy.

Studies have shown that traditional long-only portfolios can benefit from diversifying into non-correlated absolute-return strategies. For this reason, it could be appropriate to invest a portion of your money in them. Some funds, such as managed futures, tend to make money when markets get volatile, which is exactly the time when you need more diversification.

Absolute Return versus Relative Return

The vast majority of mutual funds and ETFs, and their managers, follow what's called a *relative-return strategy*. Their objective is to track with or beat a passive index, such as the S&P 500 or Barclays Aggregate Bond Index. What happens when that index goes down 50 percent? If those managers go down only 35 percent, that's considered good because they held on to fifteen more percentage points than the index did, but to the investor, that loss feels horrible.

Let's contrast that method to an absolute-return strategy. An absolute-return strategy is seeking to make money regardless of the market's direction. These managers do not have handcuffs limiting them to only buying securities. They can both buy and short sell investments, which gives them the ability to profit in up and down markets. In many cases they're not benchmarking to a particular index. There are numerous strategies that employ absolute returns by investing in a wide variety of markets. You can invest in them through mutual funds, ETFs, and public and private funds.

Absolute-Return Strategies to Consider

Although there are many types of alternative funds to consider, the following strategies are good choices that may be appropriate for long-term investors:

MANAGED FUTURES/MACRO

Macro-strategy managers trade a broad range of strategies in which the investment process is predicated on movements in underlying economic variables and the impact they have on equity, fixed income, currencies, and commodity markets. Managers employ a variety of techniques; both discretionary and systematic approaches are combined with top-down and bottom-up analysis. Quantitative and fundamental analysis is used to select opportunities for both long- and short-term holding periods.

HEDGED EQUITY

Equity-hedge strategies maintain positions both long and short in equity and equity-derivative securities. A wide variety of investment processes can be employed to arrive at an investment decision, including both quantitative and fundamental techniques. Strategies can be broadly diversified or narrowly focused on specific sectors. They can range in terms of net market exposure, leverage employed, holding period, concentrations of market capitalizations, and valuation.

EQUITY-MERGER ARBITRAGE

Merger-arbitrage strategies focus on opportunities in companies currently engaged in corporate transactions, such as mergers and acquisitions. Transactions are frequently across borders and involve multiple international regulatory institutions. Many transactions minimize exposure to corporate credit.

FIXED-INCOME ARBITRAGE

Fixed-income arbitrage managers typically employ strategies that seek to take advantage of price differentials and inefficiencies between fixed-income securities that are related either economically or statistically.

Equity-market-neutral strategies employ sophisticated quantitative techniques of analyzing price data to ascertain information about future price movement and relationships between securities. These can include both factor-based and statistical arbitrage-trading strategies. Equity-market-neutral strategies typically maintain net equity-market exposure to no greater than 10 percent long or short.

I recommend creating a comprehensive portfolio by blending these types of strategies with a traditional stock and bond portfolio. The percentage allocation to these strategies depends on your specific circumstances and needs. Before investing, discuss your plan with an experienced expert who is knowledgeable in alternative investments.

The Power of Explanatory Variables

Explanatory variables are factors that attempt to describe the underlying reasons why the markets move. They are tested for efficacy over time. Because the past does not represent the future, one must understand the underlying logic and how it relates to the current environment. If a factor has a strong logical explanation for working and shows significant statistical evidence, the variable could be used to make investment decisions.

The only relevant test of the validity of a hypothesis is comparison of prediction with experience.

—Milton Friedman

Because markets are driven by human beings, they cannot be predicted with the same accuracy as natural sciences like physics. But that's okay because investors need only a slight edge to be very successful.

One insider secret is that some of the most successful investment managers in history have correctly predicted their trades around only 30 percent of the time! In baseball terms, these managers batted about .300. How have they done this? By making much more money when they were right and by cutting losses short. Success occurs when you have strong risk management combined with robust explanatory variables.

Here are some simple examples of explanatory variables that have historically added value for investors:

Value/Mean Reversion

Warren Buffett comes to mind when most people think about value investing. The value philosophy seeks to buy inexpensive securities relative to some measure of value; for example, the price is low compared to earnings, assets, interests, and dividends. Value is *a mean-reversion* strategy because you are buying in a counter-trend fashion, hoping that prices will revert upward toward the average price at a higher level. In general, you want to buy bargains.

Over the long run, the evidence supports value as a great strategy to potentially outperform the general markets. Keep in mind that a valuation approach tends to work when you're investing with a longer time horizon of two or more years.[3]

Growth/Momentum

Research shows conclusive evidence that buying strength and selling weakness on an intermediate-term basis can outperform the markets.[4] There are two types of momentum: *cross-sectional* and *time-series*. Time-series uses past performance to predict its own future returns.[5] In contrast, cross-sectional momentum compares performance relative to peers. Trends do in fact exist in the markets, and investors should take advantage of them.

Turnover

The evidence suggests that lower turnover can be better for some asset classes, especially after taxes.[6] In large-cap stock portfolios, lower turnover tends to give better results. If the manager trades too often, it generates excessive short-term gains. Extra costs from the bid/ask spread, commissions, and the impact of trading also hurt results.

Smart investing translates from the drawing board to real life.

Expense Ratios

Investments with lower expense ratios allow you to keep more money working, and they tend to generate better returns.[7]

Downside Deviation

Lower downside deviation means the investment historically lost less money when the market went down. Those managers with lower downside deviation tend to perform better than those with high downside deviation.[8]

Active Return

Managers with higher returns than the benchmarks tend to have better results, or at least not as bad as those with a poor performance record. [9]Managers that outperform do not necessarily continue to do so, but bad performers do generally continue to perform subpar.

Don't fall into the trap of investing with storytellers who sound compelling but don't back up their approach with a systematic method. Short-term results tend to be random, but long-term outcomes are related to skill! There are many more explanatory variables that can be discussed, but they are outside the scope of this book; however, if investors focus only on the concepts listed in this book, they will be far ahead of the game.

What Is Asset Allocation?

Asset allocation is an investment strategy that attempts to balance risk versus reward by adjusting the percentage of each asset in an investment portfolio according to the investor's risk tolerance, goals, and investment time frame. It's a useful tool to determine the maximum percentages allowed for certain assets in order to keep the investor's risk in line with their tolerance for volatility.

The popularity of asset allocation rose from *modern portfolio theory* (MPT) developed by Harry Markowitz. MPT assumes that investors want to maximize their returns, given a desired level of risk. This is accomplished by a process called *mean-variance optimization* (MVO). It is a mathematical technique that uses return estimates, correlation, and variances of multiple assets to create a set of optimal portfolios called an *efficient frontier*. An optimal portfolio has the highest average return for a given level of variance.

The Misuse of Portfolio Optimization

Although MVO is appealing, it is often misused by investment professionals. Relying on historical statistics of returns, risk, and correlation in order to optimize a portfolio is naive. As you probably guessed, returns and correlation are not stable and therefore not representative of one, three, five, or ten years in the future. If you had perfect foresight using historical data, MVO would give you the perfect portfolio; however, this is unrealistic.

Because the model is very sensitive to the estimates, if future returns and risks are slightly different than the assumptions, the portfolio will perform poorly. MVO falsely assumes that returns are normally distributed like a perfect bell curve, but real market returns have *fat tails* and *discontinuities.*

Fat tails are sudden, large negative returns that occur more often than that described by a bell-curve distribution. Discontinuities means that market returns can have sudden large leaps up or plunges down, with corresponding gaps in prices. Both effects cause the model to underestimate the risk during bear markets, so negative returns from bear markets have a larger impact on portfolios than that predicted by MVO. This is why risk-management techniques are so important.

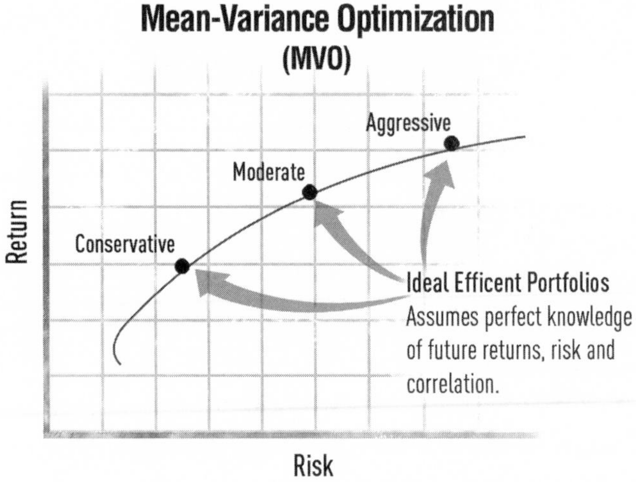

Although MVO cannot guarantee a certain level of return, nor keep losses from happening, it does provide a useful framework for making decisions. It gives investors a reasonable estimate of risk and provides a road map for blending investments for a better return/risk profile. Asset allocation is more effective when combined with fundamental and technical analysis. Investors who understand the underlying drivers of return can modify asset-allocation models to be better-suited for current opportunities available in the markets.

The main takeaway from MVO is the following:

- Diversify across asset classes that have lower correlation. Be sure the correlation differences are based not only on statistics but also fundamental drivers of returns.
- Select investments with better reward/risk ratios within each asset class.
- Allocate assets so that the overall risk is within your limits.

Benefits of Rebalancing Asset Classes

Rebalancing is a process of establishing target percentages for investments, then buying or selling when the investments stray too far away. When the allocation is out of line, rebalancing will bring them back closer to their targets. These targets are specific percentages of the portfolio. For example, you may want to have 35 percent of your portfolio in U.S. stocks. If this percentage increases to 45 percent, you might consider selling enough stocks to take their share of your portfolio back down to 35 percent. Target percentages can be applied in a broad or narrow fashion to individual securities, styles, or asset classes.

Numerous studies find that rebalancing is an effective tool to improve portfolio performance.[10] Strong evidence suggests that rebalancing outperforms buy and hold in terms of risk/reward ratios. Most of the benefit is derived from better risk control resulting in higher *Sharpe ratios* and *Sortino ratios*. One study estimated that rebalancing adds thirty-five basis points (0.35 percent) to returns. Doesn't it make sense to have a rebalancing strategy?

Rebalancing

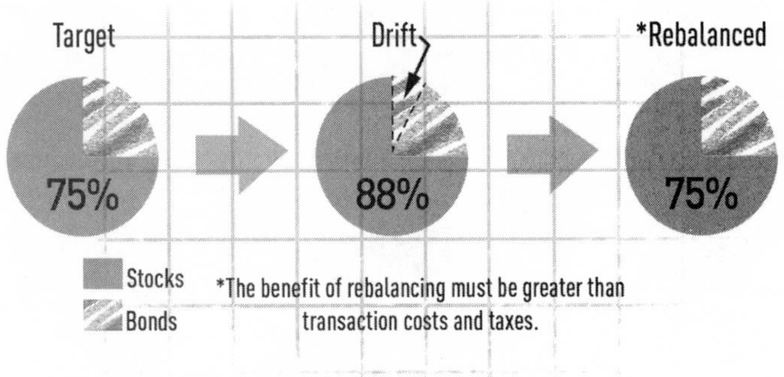

Protect Your Money 4

Wall Street has a few prudent principles; the trouble is that they are always forgotten when they are most needed.

—Benjamin Graham

In the world of finance, risk management separates the winners from the losers. It's more important than how well you select stocks or predict the markets. If you get it right, then you can pursue higher returns while you manage your downside. Risk management requires you to have rules to size your investments and, most importantly, to exit when risks are too high. There are times when you will be tempted to break your rules. This is a big no-no and usually leads to disappointment. The lack of solid risk-management guidelines is the number-one reason for poor performance; therefore, I believe it is crucial to understand your personal risk profile and to institute rigorous guidelines.

What Is Risk?

How much *volatility* are you willing to assume to pursue returns? The answer to this question is your risk tolerance. In the context of investing, risk is the chance that you could lose money. Each investment has uncertainty no matter how much research you have done. It doesn't depend on how smart you are. You can never know every aspect of your investment or perfectly predict the future. For these reasons, I believe capital should be managed to limit losses as much as possible while leaving the upside open. Limiting losses requires you to predefine your risk tolerance and convert it into measurable statistics.

Does Buy and Hold Make Sense?

Some investors believe that stocks go up over the long haul, so why not just buy and hold them and not worry about it? Although it is true that stocks in the United States have historically trended upward, there are very long periods of poor performance. This happened in the 1930s, 1970s, and the first decade of this century. Longtime periods of poor stock performance also happen in other countries. In Japan, the Nikkei 225 stock index peaked on December 29, 1989, and as of February 24, 2021, it has yet to recover. That's thirty-two years of no growth. You must have an *extremely* long time horizon to weather that type of storm. If you were a buy-and-hold investor, surely you were disappointed, and hopefully you were not retiring during that time. This is one reason why I recommend an investment plan that diversifies the source of returns and does not rely on the performance of a particular market.

It's also a big reason why I recommend investing in flexible strategies that have opportunities to profit in both up and down markets.

Do not buy the hype from Wall Street and the press that stocks always go up. There are long periods when stocks do nothing and other investments are better."

—Jim Rogers

Finding Your Comfort Zone

Since we know that fear and panic can infect our decision-making at the wrong time, it's best to set up a comfort zone that defines your risk tolerance. As we discussed, staying in your comfort zone will help you avoid a permanent capital loss. You don't want to be stuck in cash at the wrong time and then reinvest late. By the time you are comfortable enough to get back in again, chances are you already missed out on good profits. The combination of locking in a loss and making less on the way up will hurt your results. It is difficult to "get back on the horse" after you feel burned. It's just human nature.

Making up a loss is not the same as generating a gain; it's much harder to claw back from a severe loss simply because of the math. You have to earn a higher return to break even, especially the larger the loss becomes. For example, if your portfolio goes down 50 percent, you need to go up 100 percent just to break even! In this case you need to double the return of your prior loss. How many times do investments double in value, and how long will that take? Valuable time is wasted when trying to recover from an excessive loss.

Excessive market volatility truly affects our emotions. The psychological cost is brutal when we are outside our comfort zone. We can't sleep at night and we become nervous. The mental and physical pain keeps mounting to the point that our well-being is shot. The bottom line: excessive risk is really not worth potential gains.

Let's first assume that you have a sound investment strategy based on evidence. With that in place, now we can look at risk. If you don't match your risk tolerance to your investment strategy correctly, you'll lose money when you abandon a perfectly good strategy at the wrong time. You could invest a smaller amount in riskier investments and be able to withstand normal volatility. In fact, sizing your positions is the key. With the proper position size, you will keep portfolio volatility within your risk limits, be able to sit through ordinary movements, and reap the rewards of your strategy.

NEVER take more risk than your finances can withstand.

NEVER take more risk than you can psychologically endure.

ALWAYS match your goals to your risk tolerance.

You can't blame a particular type of asset for your losses when you sell at the wrong time. Actually, there is no ideal asset class or investment strategy. They all have merit when priced attractively and traded properly. As long as your plan has an edge, you can make money over the long term. Along the way, some investments will lose money. This should be expected and accounted for when estimating the best position size.

Step One: Perform a Risk Assessment

A great starting point to understand your risk profile is to take a well-designed risk assessment. I prefer using psychometric techniques that have been tested to be valid with many people. The test should compare your results to a large database of investors so you can see how your risk preference stacks up against others. It should also use statistical analysis to match your risk profile with various levels of volatility. The results should be combined with other factors related to your financial plan. Keep in mind that the risk assessment is only a single input to your overall risk picture.

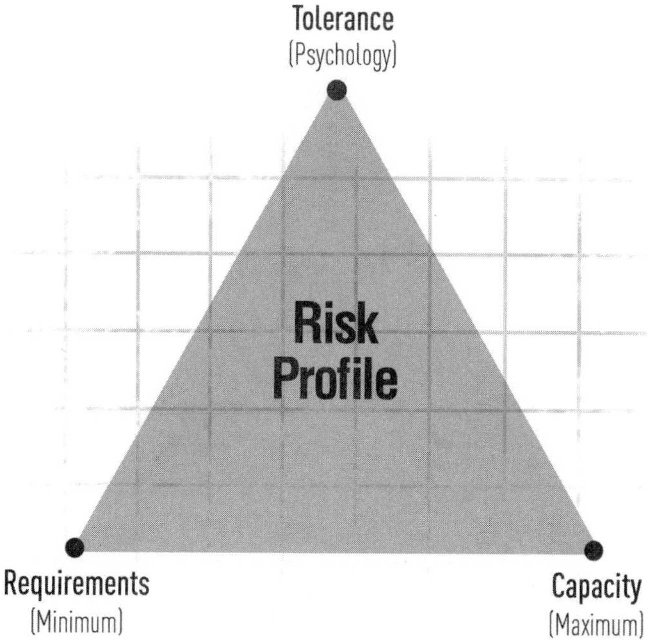

The type of risk assessment I recommend has three parts to it. The first part is to define your *risk tolerance*. This measures how much downside risk you can psychologically tolerate before you begin to get uncomfortable. The second is to determine your *risk capacity*. This measures how much risk your finances can withstand. Finally, your *risk requirement* measures how much risk you must take to earn the return needed to reach your goals. Both you and your spouse should take the risk assessment because each of you may have a different profile. Average both risk profiles to get a combined picture. You may want to use this average risk profile for constructing your portfolio.

There is a hierarchy of importance between the three risk profile measures. Here are the general rules:

- *Risk capacity rule one*—Never take more risk than your finances can withstand.
- *Risk tolerance rule two*—Never take more risk than you can psychologically endure.
- *Risk requirement mismatch rule three*—If your risk tolerance is lower than your risk requirement, you should consider adjusting your goals to be more realistic. In this case you will not likely reach your initial goals successfully because your tolerance for risk will not allow for an adequate return to build enough wealth. If you take more risk than your risk tolerance, you will likely abandon your strategy at the wrong time; therefore, it is better to adjust your goals to match your risk tolerance.

Step Two: Determine Your Key Metrics

Once you've taken the risk assessment, I recommend establishing the target measures that define your personal comfort zone. Although there are dozens of risk measures, I have found two that work exceptionally well. They are *drawdown* and *standard deviation*. The reason they work in practice is because they are easy to understand, and they coincide with your emotions.

Drawdown is the percent change in your portfolio

from peak to trough over a given time frame. It's one of the best measures of risk from a psychological standpoint because investors tend to remember the *highest* value of their accounts before a decline. The high becomes a benchmark because we feel regret as values go down. We think, *I could have sold out last month.* Define this number for yourself by asking, "What is the maximum drop in value I can bear while I'm pursuing higher returns?" Is it 10 percent, 15 percent, 25 percent, or 50 percent?

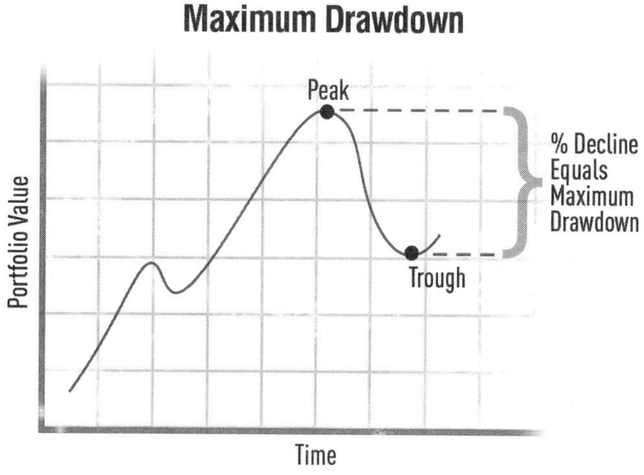

Another excellent measure is the standard deviation of returns. This measures the amount of variation around the average of returns. If there is a large amount of variation in the returns, the standard deviation will be higher. Conversely, investments that are less volatile will have a smaller standard deviation.

Standard deviation is different from drawdown because standard deviation measures *both* up and down returns, whereas drawdown only deals with negative outcomes. Combining these two numbers can help you and your advisors construct a portfolio in your comfort zone.

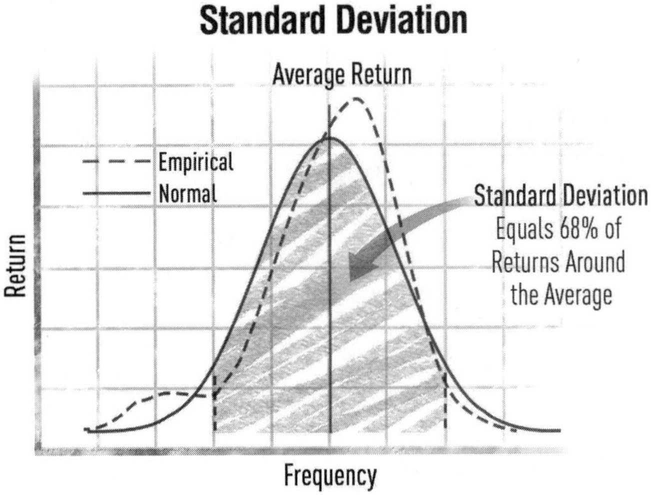

Step Three: Simulate Your Portfolio's Performance

How do you develop a portfolio within your risk tolerance? One good way is through portfolio simulation. This is a type of statistical analysis that performs thousands of what-if scenarios, given various portfolio allocations and economic forecasts.

You want to run an analysis that answers the following questions:

- If I diversify across these strategies, how would I have performed, given historical data as well as forward-looking expectations?

- How much does the portfolio fall during times of stress when correlation is converging?

- What happens to the portfolio when times are good?

This process is called a stress test. It tests how well your portfolio holds up when times are bad.

When you conduct a portfolio simulation, be sure to account for the inflows and outflows of cash that you expect. If you're taking an income stream out of your portfolio, your risk capacity is lower than if you are adding to your portfolio. For this reason, it's better to invest for lower volatility when you are pulling more money out.

This phenomenon occurs because of *reverse-dollar cost averaging*. I discuss this in detail in Chapter 9, "Common Questions."

Your feelings, friends, or Facebook should not dictate the amount of risk you take.

Solving the financial independence puzzle starts with your spending rate. This rate is the percentage of your assets that you spend in a given year. For example, if you spend $50,000 from a $1,000,000 portfolio, your spending rate is 5 percent ($50,000/$1,000,000). If you spend too rapidly, you will run out of money too soon. The key point to remember is that too much volatility lowers your sustainable spending rate, which is yet another reason to define the risk for your accounts. Portfolio simulations help you develop an asset allocation plan that can maximize the probability of achieving your objectives regardless of the market environment.

Step Four: Construct Your Portfolio

After completing your portfolio simulations, you will have a good starting point for your asset allocation strategy.

Now your portfolio can be fine-tuned for the current market conditions. Factors to consider include valuation in the markets, attractiveness of absolute-return strategies, and, perhaps, guaranteeing some of your portfolio income and principal.

You may want to overweight assets that are undervalued and underweight those that are expensive. Much of the risk inherent in a security is related to its current valuation. Let's say you invest in a high-flying stock that's really expensive.

Maybe it's a tech stock that's been going up for a long time and the price is well ahead of its earnings. That's a riskier endeavor than investing in a solid company that has a strong balance sheet and is temporarily down in price, especially if the company has a big, competitive advantage in its industry. Focusing your attention on good values is smart risk management.

For some people, it makes economic sense to guarantee a portion of their capital. Typically, this is done through insurance companies and pensions. Keep in mind that any guarantee is only as good as the creditworthiness of the issuing entity. With that said, adding guarantees can extend the life of your money and increase the probability of success.

Each person's situation is different, so you need a financial plan to see what improves your standing. You may want to invest in a guaranteed fixed annuity to supplement your Social Security benefits and pension plan. These annuities can increase your security, especially if you have a lower tolerance for risk, need steady income, and want to protect your money in case you live a long life. With that said, there are many pitfalls with annuities, and they are not for everyone. The downsides to annuities are primarily related to taxes, loss of liquidity, and high fees. I discuss the pros and cons in more detail in Chapter 9, "Common Questions."

It's not whether you're right or wrong, but how much money you make when you're right and how much you lose when you're wrong.

—George Soros

The Profit Formula Every Investor Should Know

We've discussed the bigger asset-allocation picture; now I'd like to explain how to think about making money in your individual positions within your portfolio. There is a formula that explains the profitability of *all* investors and traders.

It contains four key metrics that can be transformed into actions to improve performance. Academics call this formula *mathematical expectation* or *expected value*. The math is not complicated.

The four numbers that determine your portfolio profits are

- P(W), the probability of a winning investment;
- $(W), the average dollar win;
- P(L), the probability of a losing investment; and
- $(L), the average dollar loss.

The profit earned with any investment program is calculated with the following formula:

$$\text{Expected Profit} = [P(W) \times \$(W)] - [P(L) \times \$(L)]$$

The first number, P(W), is the percentage of your investments that make money. The next number, $(W), is the average profit you earn when you invest in a winner. Conversely, P(L) is the percentage of time you lose money, and $(L) is the average loss per losing trade.

As the formula states, the expected profit is equal to the probability of having a winning trade *times* the average profit *minus* the probability of losing *times* the average loss. It doesn't matter if you're a short-term day trader or a long-term investor like Warren Buffett. That math works for everybody.

Why is that formula important, and what does it tell you to do? The formula tells you that you want your average winner's gain to be much greater than your average loser's loss. Second, it shows you that you want to minimize both the number of your losses and the average value of each loss. How do you do that? You must predefine your initial risk *before* entering an opportunity. In other words, to minimize losses, you must determine what percentage of your capital you're willing to lose if you're wrong. ***I cannot overemphasize the importance of this.*** The only things we as investors can do is control our risk and seek explanatory variables to increase the probability of success. This approach can lean opportunity in your favor. Furthermore, let those winners ride and become as big as they possibly can before you exit them.

So, to summarize, this formula instructs you to

- limit losses;
- let your profits ride as long as possible before exiting; and

- lean the probabilities in your favor to increase your hit rate by seeking explanatory variables.

The Payoff of Risk Management

To conclude, determine your *risk tolerance, capacity,* and *requirements.* Next, establish and quantify your *comfort zone.* Use metrics to measure your risk and the risk thresholds that you can live with. What are the draw-down and standard deviation that make sense for you? Next, *stress-test* your strategy with portfolio simulation. This, in turn, provides more information to support that your portfolio risk will match your comfort zone when markets are rough. Consider including *absolute-return strategies* in your portfolio to counteract the risks of buy-and-hold strategies. You may want to *guarantee a portion of your capital* to further truncate potential downside risks. Last, keep the *valuations* in mind when investing so that you are not exposing your capital to securities in a speculative bubble.

The most important lesson from risk management is to remember to let your winners ride and to cut your losers short. The best investors and traders in the world are often right only a small percentage of the time, yet they make tremendous profits because they manage risk effectively. You can follow these same steps as well.

Big Decisions, Big Wins! 5

You become a winner the instant you decide to start living like a winner.

—Mark Minervini

In this chapter, I will discuss some of the most common big decisions you may face now or in the future. These decisions could lead to a dramatic increase in your wealth and happiness. I will focus on ways of thinking about each issue. Because tax and economic conditions change often, I will talk about the extensive overarching thought process that leads to good decisions, rather than the minute details of the rules.

In this chapter, I will discuss the five most common big decisions that can lead to big wins:

- pension income choices
- managing company stock
- concentrated investments

- relocating and moving
- inheritances

Sound thinking leads to sound actions.

Pension Income Choices

Take Control of Your Pension Income

What is a defined benefit pension plan? It is a retirement plan that is provided by the company that guarantees an income stream that can be paid for life or for a certain number of years. This guaranteed income stream is backed by the company or the government. The amount of income you receive is usually based on the number of years you worked at the firm and your salary.

Are You One of the Lucky Ones?

If you have a defined benefit pension, consider yourself extremely lucky! I have looked at my clients over the years and found that 76 percent of them have not had an opportunity to get into a pension during their lifetime. Only 24 percent of our clients have a pension!

According to CNN Money, only 14 percent of the companies in the private sector provide a pension for employees. On the other hand, 84 percent of state and local governments do provide a defined benefit plan.

But there is a big problem. Many of these plans are extremely underfunded, which means the employers don't have the necessary funds to pay for the promised income to employees. This calls into question whether or not you will actually receive your promised income stream because the system is stressed. It's very likely that the federal and state governments will have to raise taxes to get the money they need to pay the pension income in the future. What makes matters worse, if interest rates remain low and the stock market delivers a lower return, even more money will be raised through higher taxation. It is either higher taxes or lower compensation. This could be very difficult in the future for both government and private sector employees.

Disadvantages of Taking Pension Income

The main advantage of your defined benefit plan is that it makes it easier for you to budget during retirement.

Having a steady fixed income stream can give you comfort and may lower the risk of your overall plan. The income stream is also guaranteed by the Pension Benefit Guarantee Corporation (PBGC).

On the other hand, there are many potential disadvantages of taking the income stream from your pension rather than investing a lump sum.

Here are just a few:

- You have no say in how your money is invested.

- If your employer gets into trouble, you may receive substantially less money even though the income is guaranteed by the PBGC.

- Many companies are underfunded to meet their current obligations, much less the future increases needed.

- If you take the income, you cannot take a lump sum in the future. This gives you substantially less flexibility.

- The rate of return in most pensions has been very low due to low interest rates.

- The quality of your lifestyle can be worse over time because your pension income does not keep up with inflation.

- Once you decide about your payout with your pension income, you are locked into the contract and cannot change it.

- Because the income stream is based on how long you live, your benefit can be substantially less, especially if you allow your spouse to get a benefit after you pass.

The Silver Lining Could Be a Lump Sum Rollover to Your IRA

Many companies are giving employees the option to take a lump sum instead of the income stream over time. Because of all the disadvantages, it usually makes sense to do an analysis to find out if you are more likely to be better off taking the lump sum versus the income stream. Because most companies do not want to continue having the huge obligation of a pension, they would rather pay you more to take the lump sum. When I say, "pay you more," I mean the expected return implied in the lump sum could be larger than the return when you take the income over time. It makes sense to compare the returns of each option.

You may be better off rolling your pension into your IRA and taking control of your future. To find out, compare your return expected from taking an income stream versus taking a lump sum.

Managing Company Stock

Company Stock

Most employers are no longer providing a defined benefit income pension; instead, they are compensating employees with company stock and matching contributions to 401(k) plans. Many firms believe that everyone will be better off if employees become owners of the firm through stock ownership. This gives employees a piece of the upside in profits, and hopefully gives employees the incentive to help the firm prosper. For most management teams, company stock compensation appears to be a better option than paying high fixed-pension and administration costs.

It is up to you to maximize your company stock and invest in your 401(k) retirement plan wisely.

You can acquire company stock in various ways. Typically, you either buy it at a discount, get an option to buy it, or are granted stock outright. You could get rich with company stock if the company is doing well.

You may want to know how much company stock you should buy. The amount to invest depends on many factors, but here are the most important:

- Is the company publicly traded and growing fast?
- Are you able to buy at a substantial discount to current market prices?
- Does the company have financial stability, including plenty of cash and low debt?

- Is the company in a well-defined niche in the marketplace, resulting in a competitive advantage over the competition?
- Are there strong growth trends in the industry that can last for a long time to sustain the growth?
- How much are you paying for the stock, and is the company a good value compared to earnings, assets, and growth?
- Is the management team making good decisions to allocate capital for growth and investor returns?
- Is management running the operation well?
- Are there better opportunities for your funds that could benefit your overall financial picture?

A stock that is down can go down further. A stock that goes up can go higher.

Type of Company Stock Plans

When you move up the corporate ladder, you are likely to have different stock compensation plans available to you. Here is a spoiler alert: you probably will be shocked by how much tax you will pay to get your stock. If you work for a highly successful company and you make a lot of money from company stock, just resolve that you will have to pay a lot in taxes. There are ways to mitigate this, but not entirely. Just understand, if you make a lot of money, you are probably going to pay a lot of taxes eventually.

There are six basic kinds of stock compensation plans: stock options, restricted stock, restricted stock units (RSUs), stock appreciation rights, phantom stock, and employee stock purchase plans. Each kind of plan provides you with terms for price and taxation. It's very important to make sure you understand the terms of the plans available to you.

Participate and profit from the stock plan that gives you the highest return after tax.

Don't Let Tax Worries Kill Your Net Worth

The biggest blunder I've seen with people that make a lot of money in company stock is they can let tax concerns kill their net worth. You may avoid selling your stock when it makes sense to, just because you want to avoid taxes. When things go wrong for a company, stock prices usually fall A LOT faster than they rose.

In those cases, you can find yourself with less than half of your nest egg in a blink of an eye.

Don't get so hung up on taxes that you lose sight of the objective truth about your company's future.

Objectivity Is Key

Objectivity is the most important attribute needed when making decisions about your stock. If you lose *objectivity*, you might make the mistake of holding on too long and then lose tremendous amounts of money. I have watched people hold company stock, get married to the company, and lose big. When the company prospects got worse, they held onto it, and they lost tremendous amounts of their wealth.

Get an Outside Perspective

When you work for a company that you love, and you're making a lot of money, it's easy to lose perspective. I find it absolutely crucial that you seek an outside perspective from smart people. Management and other employees within your firm may be biased and not see the truth about the future prospects of your company. Outside perspectives can give you a better understanding about what's going on with competitors, how expensive or inexpensive the stock is relative to its cash flow, the safety of the financials, and what level of risk you have to your overall plan. The overarching rule is ***think about your entire financial picture***.

Concentrated Investment

How to Manage a Concentrated Stock Position

This leads to the nuances of managing a concentrated investment position so that you can participate in the upside while managing your downside. It is a balancing act with no perfect decision. Even the smartest executives rarely get the absolute top or bottom in their trades. Think long term and how you will manage the big picture of your financial plan.

If you get too concentrated in a stock, no matter how great the company is, it could have a devastating impact on your future.

Here are my general guidelines for managing a concentrated position:

- Am I financially secure right now, even if the stock goes to zero?
- Is the stock greater than 20 percent of my net worth?

- Is the stock overvalued based on earnings, growth, and net assets?
- How much of any stock I sell would be taxable gains?
- Are my profits considered capital gains or ordinary income?
- What is my current tax bracket?
- Will I be subject to alternative minimum tax (AMT)?
- Which lot of shares can I sell that would have the lowest tax impact?
- Is the stock in an uptrend, consolidating sideways, or beginning to break into a downtrend technically?
- If I am concerned about the stock going down because of a change in the prospects, should I sell or hedge?

Don't overconcentrate in your company's stock.

Try to diversify. You probably won't sell your stock at the highest value.

What really matters is that you protect your financial security.

Then, move on with your life.

Move to a New State and Prosper

One of the biggest decisions you may have to make is whether to move to a new state. The location you choose could have a big positive impact on your future.

Lower Your Taxes and Cost of Living

There are many reasons why you might consider a new location rather than staying put. You may save big money if you live in certain states with lower taxes and fewer regulations. You may be able to keep your current high-paying job and work remotely in a lower cost-of-living environment. I have found that many people can lower their tax bill considerably if they move to a lower-taxed state.

These lower-taxed states may also have a lower cost of living because the price of groceries, fuel, healthcare, and housing are inexpensive compared to your current home state. If you are able to keep your current income level and lower your costs, this allows you to save more and improve your financial situation.

Convert Some of Your Home Equity to Cash

One of the biggest financial reasons to move is to convert some of the equity in your current home into liquid investments. These investments can then provide future income or be a nest egg for emergencies. If you have much of your savings tied up in retirement accounts, you may be faced with a large tax bill in the future. Retirement accounts are taxed heavily if you need a lump sum for a big purchase or medical emergencies. It is important to keep a large amount of money in liquid assets as you age because there are a lot of unknowns that require cash. Given that there is a tremendous amount of uncertainty in our economy, having liquid sources of assets is very important as well. If you live in a house that's worth more money than a newly purchased residence, you could sell your house and pocket the difference in an investment account that is liquid. You may have taxes to pay if you do this, depending on the rules in place at the time. You may also be able to make the transaction without taxes.

Provide More Flexibility

Having more liquidity can improve your situation dramatically during retirement. It will give you more flexibility in how you withdraw money out of your retirement accounts in later years. This can lower your tax bill over time because you have tax diversification. You can manage which account you take income from year-by-year as the tax laws change.

Another reason you may want to move is because you want to be closer to your relatives. You may find yourself much happier being closer to family and friends that are far from you now. Improved relationships lead to improved happiness.

If you live in a cold climate, moving to a warmer climate can improve your ability to be more active in your later years.

This could lower your stress level, and may help you live a longer life because you are able to live a healthier, active lifestyle. If the new location you consider is full of activities that you enjoy, this is even more of a positive for you.

What Hinders a Move

There are some thoughts that can hinder you from making that decision to move to a new state, even though it makes a lot of sense. A fear of the unknown can overwhelm you if you focus your attention on fear-based self-talk. For example, you may continually ask yourself, "What if I don't like the new location? I don't want to have to make all new friends and change my routine. I don't want the hassle of finding new people."

Here are a few tips that may help you decide if you should make the move:

- Compare the cost of living, taxes, and home prices to your current home state. Do you have a net gain or loss from the move financially?

- Assess how much money you have in liquid assets. If you have most of your money tied up in illiquid assets, you will gain more financial flexibility if you sell your home and invest the proceeds in stocks and bonds that are more accessible. This could lower your tax bill later on because if you need money down the road, you won't be forced to withdraw money from highly taxed retirement accounts.

- Take a vacation to the locations that you find interesting. Try to stay longer and envision what your lifestyle would be if you lived there. Where would you live, shop, or meet other people? If that is still an option, maybe you can rent a house or apartment on a short-term lease while you feel out the area. You may find that you love the place and are ready to pounce. Then you can sell your existing home and move. Or you may decide you want to explore new areas to move to.

- If you have been thinking about a move, go ahead and see if a move makes sense for you. Moving to a new location could be the best thing for your life.

Inheritances

Do the Right Thing with Your Inheritance

If your parents or a loved one left you an inheritance, you may be overwhelmed with many big decisions. This is your opportunity to make smart choices and feel comfortable with your moves.

Here are some tips that benefit you if you get an inheritance:

- Plan your moves; do not rush because you have many decisions to make.

- Recognize that emotional attachment can get in the way of good decisions.

- You probably will be better off consolidating your accounts.

- Change the investment allocation to meet your goals, not the decedent's goals.

- Seek the advice of a team that can collaborate with you—including a financial advisor, CPA, and attorney.

I will focus on how to think about managing your inheritance, rather than the specifics of the rules, because rules change very often. There are usually many emotions that overwhelm a person who receives an inheritance.

Depending on how you grew up, and your self-talk about money, you could be predisposed to make bad choices. Self-awareness is key.

Understand that if you are grieving, it's important to give yourself some time to regain your balance before you make big decisions. You may be forced to make some big decisions, but try to defer them if you can. Talk to both family members AND trusted advisors that are experts. Remember that family members may not be experts in a complicated area of finance.

It may be difficult to gather all the information that you need to fully understand your current situation. Even if there was a good estate plan put in place by the deceased, you may have assets that are titled in many ways that will need to be retitled. It's important to get them retitled in the proper fashion, and it's important to make sure that you do not incur excessive taxes in the process. The best way to get this accomplished is to work with a team of qualified advisors who are fiduciaries, a certified public accountant, and a lawyer. The combination of these three experts in collaboration will give you the best result.

It helps most people to consolidate their accounts so they align with their goals. When you consolidate accounts, you get more clarity about where your money is located and how it will be used for your goals. You will have a better understanding of your overall picture and how it is invested. A streamlined financial picture can also help your advisors analyze your tax situation.

You probably will find that your inherited investments are not aligned with your goals. The deceased probably had their investments aligned to their goals. The design was for their income, growth, liquidity, and tax situation.

Now that this is your money, it's time to rebalance your portfolio to your own plan.

During the process of realigning your investments, you will need to consider the tax implications and the return and risk characteristics of what you own. Unless you are an expert in the investment world, I advise working with a Chartered Financial Analyst (CFA) or similar investment professional to help you *before* you make trading decisions.

A good advisor will help you develop the next step to create your investment policy for your own situation. Once you've accomplished your own strategy, then it's a matter of going from point A to point B. Be sure to look out for unnecessary capital gains or taxable income distributions. This often happens when you cash out of certain assets.

You may be taxed 100 percent as income, or incur short-term gains. Try to avoid this situation if you can incorporate existing assets from your inheritance into your portfolio.

The bottom line: don't rush it. Put together the right advisors that work together with you, and don't do it alone.

Keep Your Hands Out of My F@cking Pockets!

6

We contend that for a nation to try to tax itself into prosperity is like a man standing in a bucket and trying to lift himself up by the handle.

—Winston S. Churchill

Taxes are the biggest drag on wealth creation. They take a chunk out of your money and extend the amount of time needed to build your nest egg. Your goal is to reach financial independence as quickly as possible and to keep it for the rest of your life. Anything that keeps you from that goal must be reduced or eliminated. Let's take a quick look at an example of how taxes affect wealth creation.

Taxes Slow Down Wealth Creation

Let's say you have an investment of $500,000, and let's assume the middle tax bracket is 28 percent. If you're going to invest for twenty years and your gross return is 6 percent before taxes, you're only going to *really* earn 4.32 percent because you're paying taxes out [6% × (100% – 28%) = 4.32%]. That's a reduction in your return of 1.68 percentage points per year. That doesn't sound like a lot, but let's look at what happens over the twenty-year investment period.

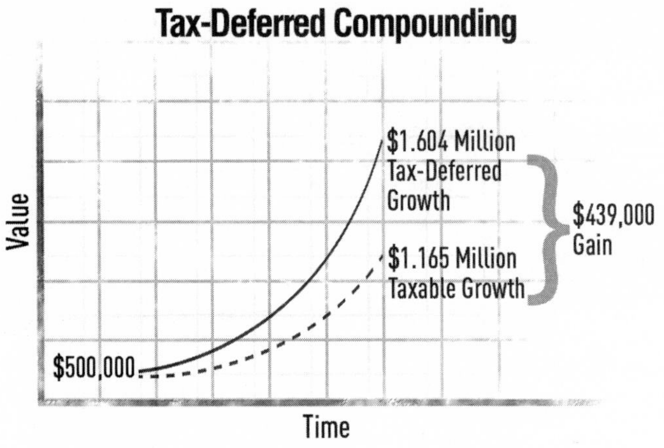

After twenty years, that taxable investment is worth $1.165 million. That sounds pretty good, but compare that to what you could earn if you invested in a tax-deferred account.

A tax-deferred account would be worth $1.604 million, an increase of $439,000. That's a huge difference that could help you achieve financial freedom faster. Taxes do matter.

You can't control Washington directly, but you can control your own actions.

You must proactively and legally avoid taxes, or your wealth will vanish quickly.

Managing your future tax bills is just as important as lowering your current ones. Taxes in the future could rise for the so-called wealthy because of irresponsible government spending. If you look at the 2021 government-spending projections, the total appropriation spending in the United States is about $4.79 *trillion* according to the Congressional Budget Office.[11] The debt burden in the United States is about $26.48 trillion.[12] That's about $80,000 per US citizen. We have ballooning spending programs that will almost certainly continue to increase, like healthcare, Social Security, Medicare, and many others.

Government spending continues to become a larger part of our overall economy. Somebody must pay for this. Who is it going to be?

Who will pay for the huge debt burden that is piling up in the United States as a result of deficit spending by the government? Is it going to be the rich? Even if we tax the rich at 100 percent, they can't pay it all off. We have to go down the pay scale to the middle class to find the money. Even if we paid off the government debt, the deficit would still continue to grow simply because we spend more than we bring in. As of 2021, deficit spending is $1.083 trillion according to the CBO. So, what can you do about this?

You can't control Washington directly, but you can control your own actions by becoming more proactive. The first step is to take advantage of tax-deferred and tax-free accounts.

Tax-deferred accounts allow you to reduce taxable income in the current year by deducting contributions to them. What's even more powerful is that you don't pay taxes on your earnings (interest, dividends, and capital gains) until you take possession or withdraw money. When you take possession of that money in later years, your withdrawals are considered taxable income; therefore, you will pay income taxes at your marginal income-tax rate, which is higher than the applicable capital-gains tax rate for many people. When you reach the age of seventy-two, you *must* take mandatory distributions, which are also taxed. Some tax-deferred accounts, such as annuities, do not require mandatory withdrawals.

You can also invest in tax-free accounts. In a tax-free account you *never* pay taxes on your earnings in the future, but you *lose* the tax deduction for contributions in the current year. If your income is high, you may not qualify for a Roth IRA because the IRS phases out your eligibility based on your modified adjusted gross income. You may have a tax-free feature in your company's retirement plan, which could be a better option because the income limits may not apply to you. This allows high-income earners to protect future returns against taxes.

It pays to see your options and then optimize and balance your contributions between tax-deferred and tax-free accounts. Although tax-deferred accounts are great for reducing taxes, it's important to avoid locking up too much money in them. You could lose important flexibility if a large portion of your wealth is in IRAs and 401(k) accounts, because those accounts are not easily accessible without tax and/or penalty consequences. Which accounts are tax-deferred or tax-free? The typical tax-deferred accounts are 401(k), 403(b), and 457 plans, plus tax-deferred annuities.

Tax-free accounts are normally Roth IRAs, 529s, and certain types of insurance policies. It's essential to have a balance.

Reduce the Cost of Capital Gains

Another strategy to lower taxes is to focus on investments with lower turnover and a longer time horizon. This generates long-term as opposed to short-term capital gains. As a result, investors with fewer short-term gains will lower their tax bills because short-term gains are taxed as income, which tends to be taxed at a higher rate.

The accounting method used to calculate your capital gains can also affect the amount of taxes you pay. You will want to use *most favorable tax-lot* accounting to minimize gains.

There are four common types of tax-lot accounting:

- first in, first out
- last in, first out
- specific lot
- average cost

First in-first out accounting assumes that your cost basis is your first lot purchased. The *last in-first out* method selects the last shares purchased to be the first to be sold. In *specific lot*, you get to choose which lot will be your cost basis. The average cost basis method simply uses the average cost. Tax-managed strategies should be able to automatically do this accounting to lower your capital gains taxes. Also, a good accountant can help figure out which method is best for you.

Another way to lower capital gains taxes is to *do tax loss harvesting* and *replacement* before the end of the tax year. It is a simple technique of selling less desirable investments for a loss in order to offset gains from another holding. Sell only investments that are not attractive or that can be replaced with similar investments. You can replace the investments sold for loss purposes with similar investments that may potentially perform better in the future.

You may have heard of *municipal bonds*. These bonds pay tax-free interest and can be an excellent investment for high-income individuals. It is a good idea to compare the yields of tax-free municipal bonds with those of taxable bonds to figure out which one will offer the best return after taxes. To compare them, you must adjust the bond yields for taxes. The one that pays the higher after-tax yield is a better buy, all else being equal. Evaluate the yield-to-maturity of bonds that have a similar credit quality and maturities to make an apples-to-apples comparison.

Comparison of Yields

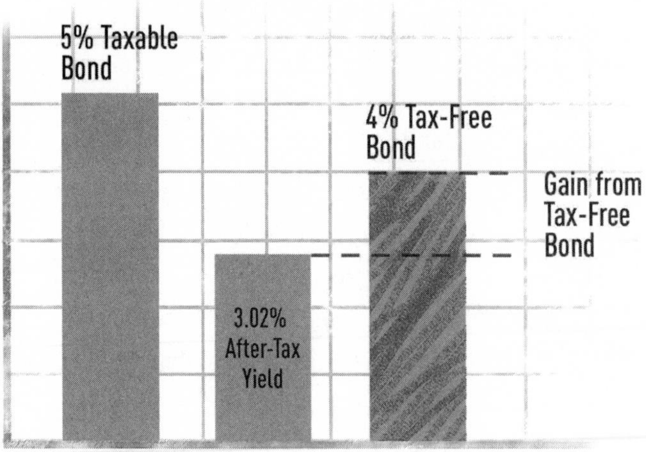

Let's say you have a taxable bond that's paying 5 percent and your current marginal tax bracket is 39.6 percent. After taxes, your yield is only 3.02 percent [5% × (100% – 39.6%)]. That's almost two full percentage points knocked off your yield because of taxes. If you can buy a bond paying 4 percent tax-free, then you will earn almost a full percentage point higher than with the taxable bond. In this case you would go with the tax-free bonds.

Avoid Paying Taxes on Other People's Gains!

You may not be aware of the *phantom tax*, a relatively unknown nuisance that causes people to pay taxes on capital gains they never actually earned. What you don't know *can* hurt you. Mutual funds have potential capital gains the moment you buy them, and if you are not careful, they can burn you. To see if your funds can affect you, check the potential capital-gains statistics tracked by mutual-fund data suppliers like Morningstar. This figure represents gains built up in the fund that have not been realized as taxable. If a fund has a high percentage of assets that were exposed to capital gains before you bought in, you may have to pay taxes if the fund manager sells the securities. If the fund goes down after you invested, then it is possible you will pay taxes even though you have a personal loss. To avoid this, put highly taxable mutual funds in non-taxable accounts or invest in a different fund that is tax efficient.

Put the Right Investments in the Right Accounts

This brings us to *asset location*. Certain investments generate more taxes than others. For this reason, it's better to put highly taxable investments in non-taxable accounts. Vanguard did an interesting study analyzing the impact on returns based purely on placing highly taxable investments in tax-deferred or tax-free accounts and locating investments with lower taxes in taxable accounts.[13] They estimated that this strategy alone could increase annual returns by 0.75 percent. If you have both types of accounts, it makes sense to determine which investments are highly taxable so you can place them in non-taxable accounts. The investments that don't have as much tax exposure can be traded in your taxable accounts.

Extend Your Income with Withdrawal Strategies

When you take money out of your portfolio, you want it to last as long as possible to preserve your lifestyle and maximize the assets that you pass on to heirs.

The order in which you take funds from various accounts can have a significant impact on how long your assets will last because of taxes.

Certain withdrawals must be taken out annually, leaving you no control over the timing of those withdrawals. For example, at age seventy-two, the mandatory required minimum distributions from your tax-deferred accounts must be withdrawn to avoid penalties. But once you've taken mandatory distributions out, which account is next? In most cases it's your taxable accounts. By taking funds from your taxable accounts first, your other assets grow at a higher after-tax return because they are tax-deferred. This extends the life of your wealth.

Once you have exhausted your taxable accounts, the next accounts to withdraw from depends on what you think is going to happen to your marginal tax bracket in the future. If you think your marginal tax bracket is going to increase, then it makes sense to take money out of your tax-deferred accounts first, then out of your tax-free accounts. If you expect your marginal tax bracket to go down in the future, then do the opposite. Take out the tax-free money first, then the tax-deferred money. For the average investor, this strategy can add up to an estimated 0.70 percent.[14]

Diversify your tax structure to avoid giving your money to the wrong people, because rules are constantly changing.

Withdrawal Order

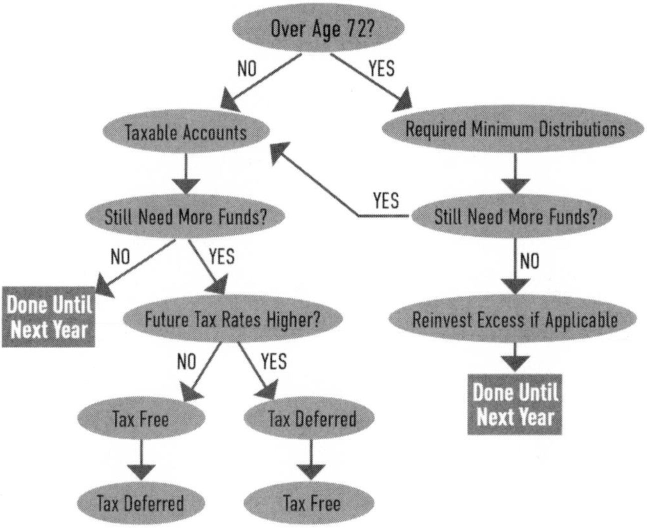

I've outlined eight basic tax-reducing strategies you can use:

1. Optimize tax-deferred and tax-free accounts.
2. Reduce capital gains taxes with longer-term strategies.
3. Use tax-loss harvesting and replacement.
4. Buy tax-free municipal bonds.
5. Use proper tax-lot accounting.
6. Avoid phantom taxes.

7. Optimize asset-location strategies.

8. Follow order-of-withdrawal guidelines.

When you use effective tax strategies, you're going to build wealth faster. Because rules change every year, it is important for you to work with a CPA or other tax advisor that keeps up with rules that affect you. One word of caution: sometimes it does not pay to have an elaborate account structure and entities established solely for tax purposes. If a loophole becomes too profitable, the government usually closes it up. Don't get too clever with tax planning. This can cause more headaches down the road. The simple tax strategies discussed in this chapter are great methods to start saving taxes.

Should I Pay Off My Mortgage?

7

A formal manipulator in mathematics often experiences the discomforting feeling that his pencil surpasses him in intelligence.

—Howard W. Eves

Have you ever wondered if you should pay off your mortgage? For decades the common wisdom has been to be debt-free before you retire. For many people, this is a wise decision, and for others, not so much. This chapter discusses the benefits and costs of paying off your mortgage.

The Worry of Debt

Recently a high-net-worth individual who has significant wealth in liquid assets asked me that question because she was worried about the economy and world politics. There is an increased sense of security when you are debt-free. She sat down with me and voiced her concern. She said, "I'm really feeling unsure about the economy. I'm seeing a lot of craziness in the world. I see governments that seem to be acting irrationally. I'm worried about war. I'm worried about the stock market going down and volatility going up. What if the Federal Reserve raises interest rates? I'm just not feeling secure even though I have some money and investments, so I want to know: should I pay off my mortgage?"

The Math Behind Your Decision

From a mathematical standpoint, the decision is based on three primary factors:

- interest rates
- your marginal tax rate
- your risk profile

The interest rate on your loan combined with your tax rate determines your after-tax cost of mortgage debt. For most people, when mortgage rates are low, it generally *does not* make sense to pay off a mortgage. The converse is also true: when rates are high, it *does* make sense to pay off the mortgage. The higher your tax bracket, the lower your after-tax costs of debt because you are getting a tax break from deducting interest expense. Let's go through the general procedure.

You may be better off financially to keep your mortgage when you retire, but you may not be able to sleep at night with the debt. There is a trade-off between economics and emotions to have a mortgage.

An intuitive way to solve the mortgage-payoff problem is to compare two projections of your net worth. The first scenario assumes you keep your mortgage, and the second scenario assumes you pay it off. Whichever projection gives you the highest net worth tells you which is better. Of course, this assumes you want to maximize your net worth. To answer this question, we generally recommend running a financial model that calculates the principal and interest payments month by month. This allows you to get a more accurate picture of the time-value of money and the use of your capital.

The Tax Impact Is Critical

It's necessary to analyze the tax benefit that you'll receive from being able to deduct your interest expense each year. When you have a mortgage, your interest payments may be deductible if you itemize your deductions. If you're in a higher tax bracket, you get more tax benefits from a mortgage than if you are in a lower tax bracket. Keep in mind that if you pay off that mortgage, the tax benefit from deducting your interest goes away, so it's critical to consider that tax benefit. Here are the steps to solve the mortgage-payoff challenge.

STEP ONE:
CALCULATE THE NET AFTER-TAX BENEFIT FROM NOT HAVING TO PAY A MORTGAGE ANYMORE

When your mortgage is gone, the real long-term benefit is you don't have to make payments any longer. On the other hand, you're paying more taxes because you lost your interest tax deductions. The net after-tax benefit that you receive can be invested or spent. To find the economic benefit of this, we compound and reinvest the after-tax cash flow on a monthly basis. Of course, because you're earning money on the reinvestment of funds over time, you have to pay some taxes on the reinvestment of earnings as well.

STEP TWO:
CALCULATE THE NET AFTER-TAX OPPORTUNITY LOSS FROM THE FUNDS USED TO PAY OFF THE MORTGAGE

Next, we answer the question, "Had I kept that money and invested it, how much would it have grown over time?" We turn our attention to the loss of earnings you will experience if you use a lump sum to pay off the mortgage. That money is no longer available to compound and grow. The economic value of this can be significant depending on your rate of return and the tax considerations. This is an opportunity loss from the investments that you're foregoing, because you could have taken the money that you paid off the mortgage with and just kept it invested.

STEP THREE: COMPARE YOUR NUMBERS

We compare the number calculated from step one to that of step two. Which gives you a better net worth? Is the benefit from not having to pay the mortgage greater than the opportunity loss from your investments? When you run through the math month by month, you get a more accurate picture to see which choice is better. Generally speaking, if the after-tax rate of return on your investments is greater than the after-tax cost of your debt, you should not pay off your mortgage, and vice versa.

Another way to look at this situation is to use the following formula:

> Net Benefit = Present Value You *Get* – Present Value You *Give Up*

In this case, you *get* the benefit from no more mortgage payments, and you give up the investment earnings over time from the lump sum used to pay off the debt.

Real-World Example

Let's look at a real example using this client's information. She didn't have a very large mortgage on her house. It was about $250,000, and the interest rate on her mortgage was under 4 percent. (See Table 1.)

Her estimated marginal tax bracket was 25 percent. We wanted to compare paying her mortgage off, assuming two different investments returns. These returns were used as discount rates to calculate the time-value of money. One is more conservative at 6 percent, and the other is more aggressive at 8 percent. The returns were netted out for taxes at her marginal tax rate. She had recently refinanced, so she had a thirty-year mortgage.

Here are the results of the calculations. Because she would no longer have a mortgage, the future value from step one is estimated to be a gain over time of about $770,327 if she earns 6 percent and $1,014,046 if she earns 8 percent. This is the future value of the reinvestment of the mortgage payments that she saves, less the increase in taxes due to the loss of a tax deduction.

Now, compare that to the investment-earnings loss, also known as opportunity costs, of $954,042 at 6 percent and $1,684,229 at 8 percent. Over time, in this particular client's case, there's actually a negative impact on her net worth of $183,715 at 6 percent or $670,183 at 8 percent, when calculated over thirty years. This example does support the idea that a short-term worry may negatively impact net worth over the long term.

Table 1. Cost/Benefit of Mortgage Payoff

	6% Gross Return	8% Gross Return
Mortgage Value Today	$250,000	$250,000
Mortgage Interest Rate	3.63%	3.63%
Marginal Tax Rate	25.00%	25.00%
Gross Return	6.00%	8.00%
After-Tax Return	4.50%	6.00%
Term	30	30
Benefit from No More Mortgage Payments	$770,327	$1,014,046
Opportunity Loss from Investments	$954,042	$1,684,229
Impact on Net Worth	($183,715)	($670,183)

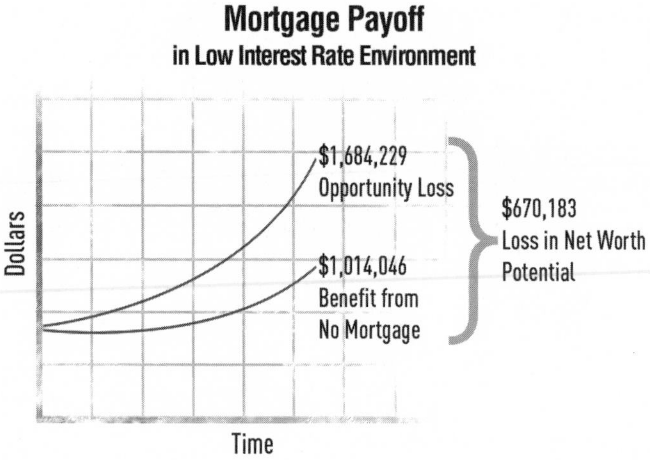

We've talked about the reasons to not pay off a mortgage, so let's discuss the reasons *for* paying it off. If your risk tolerance is low enough that your investment returns are likely to be below the after-tax cost of your mortgage, then you should pay off your mortgage. To evaluate whether this applies to you, I recommend calculating the break-even return that your investments must earn to overcome the burden of having a mortgage. This is the rate of return that, if earned, would not give you a benefit or loss when compared to paying the mortgage off or not. In this case, the breakeven return is 4.82 percent. This assumes steady compounding with no volatility in returns.

In the real world, returns are variable and move up and down. It's a good idea to perform a sophisticated analysis called a *Monte Carlo simulation* to estimate the probability of having a return lower than what is required to break even. I recommend getting Monte Carlo scenarios done for you with a financial advisor. This analysis should consider many different economic scenarios and ranges of returns. In 2021's environment, with the S&P 500's dividend yield about 1.52 percent, you only have to have a relatively small growth rate in earnings and/or multiple expansions to overcome this relatively low hurdle rate, but there is no guarantee that an account will earn a return.

When you do pay off the mortgage, one thing that's really important is that you no longer have a steady payment that you have to plan for. If you're living off your investments—you're financially independent—you may have to make your investment portfolio a little less volatile so that you could fund a steady mortgage payment that must go out. This method generally lowers your expected return and may make it more advisable to pay off the mortgage.

Consider Your Margin of Safety

If you have significantly more money invested than you owe on your mortgage, this gives you a cushion to weather the storm and to invest for the long term.

If you have a big enough margin of safety, it does not make sense to pay off your mortgage as long as your expected returns outweigh your cost of debt.

Choose the Right Advisors 8

An investment in knowledge pays the best interest.
—Benjamin Franklin

With so many different types of advisors, it can be difficult to distinguish between them. This chapter will provide information you can use to interview and find a knowledgeable, experienced advisor who can deliver valuable advice.

There are many different reasons why you come to the realization that you need a financial advisor. You may be nearing retirement and in need of a sound investment strategy to provide income for life. You may have recently received a large sum of money or have gone through a major life event, such as a marriage, a divorce, the birth of a child, or the death of a spouse. It's really hard to overcome financial challenges and to move forward if you are dissatisfied with your advisors and it seems like your progress is stunted. If you are busy in your career and want to spend quality time with your family, your time is invaluable, which creates a need to work with a trusted person.

What Should an Advisor Do for You?

Let's discuss some of the ways an advisor can be of value to you.

Find Best-of-Breed Solutions

An advisor should sort through the complex maze of financial issues in the world today. When you consider that there are thousands of exchange-traded funds, mutual funds, and stocks, it becomes a daunting task to select which investments are suitable for you. A competent advisor will have tools, techniques, and strategies that systematically screen and evaluate the alternatives available to find the best-of-breed solutions. An advisor should have a robust process to evaluate the performance and people behind the scenes of every investment he recommends to you to ensure stability. Your advisor should take this information and customize each piece to meet your unique goals.

Be a Trusted Sounding Board

A competent investment advisor will help you stay on track and give valued input. She should participate with you in making big decisions that could impact your life. She should anticipate what could happen and help you avoid costly mistakes. This alone could be worth many times the fees paid. A good advisor is also a behavioral coach that understands your attitudes toward risk. She will understand what is happening in the market and help you make better choices.

Your Advisor Must Put You First

I believe that most people are better served working with advisors that are *fiduciaries* as opposed to agents.

Advisors that work for broker-dealers, banks, and insurance companies are typically agents. Those advisors are working for the companies that employ them, and they are legally acting on behalf of their firms.

Then there are the independent registered investment advisors *who work for you*. This is a big difference.

An independent investment advisor acts as a fiduciary, so his main duty is to work in your best interest.

Competent financial advisors do more than crunch numbers; they are a mix of economists, traders, AND therapists.

—Elisa Llanes

Independent registered investment advisors have a legal and fiduciary obligation to their clients as mandated by the firm's regulatory authority and the Investment Advisor Act of 1940. Some of the obligations that the Securities and Exchange Commission (SEC) imposes, for example, on investment advisory firms include:

- acting in the best interest of their clients;
- fully disclosing all fees associated with their services and how those fees are charged;
- fully disclosing whether the firm or the employee of the firm has an affiliation with a broker-dealer or any other insurance professionals or issuers; and
- fully disclosing any facts that might cause the firm to render advice that is not disinterested.

Registered firms must complete and file with the SEC a form, *Uniform Application for Investment Adviser Registration* (ADV), that contains information about its advisors and operations, discloses information related to disciplinary matters, and contains other key disclosures. This form must be made available to clients, and you should review it before you hire a financial advisor.

There are many different financial advisor designations. For investment advice, the gold-standard credential is the *Chartered Financial Analyst* (CFA). No financial professional credential is as rigorously focused on investment knowledge as the CFA designation. Only investment professionals who demonstrate ethical, professional, and educational excellence earn the CFA charter. CFA charter holders must have at least three years of experience as an investment professional and have passed three extensive examinations. CFA charter holders have specialized education in finance, economics, and accounting as it relates to valuing investments and managing portfolios.

There is also the *Certified Financial Planner* (CFP) designation. The CFP curriculum covers a diverse body of knowledge to prepare an advisor to face clients. Individuals who have earned a CFP designation have completed an education program and passed a two-day, ten-hour examination in the United States (or a one-day, six-hour exam in Canada). The curriculum includes financial, insurance, tax, and retirement-planning courses.

The *Certified Public Accountant* (CPA) has specialized education in accounting and tax. The curriculum includes auditing, business accounting, financial accounting and reporting, tax, and regulations. These individuals may be a great companion advisor to a CFA or CFP to coordinate your taxes year by year.

The *Chartered Financial Consultant* (ChFC) and *chartered life underwriting* (CLU) designations are involved primarily in the insurance industry. The ChFC designation was created in 1982 for financial advisors who offer financial planning services to clients. It is awarded by the American College of Financial Services. Insurance agents in the United States are licensed by the states in which they work to sell and provide advice about insurance products, such as life insurance, disability insurance, and annuities.

The *Chartered Market Technician* (CMT) designation is awarded to individuals who pass three exams offered by the Market Technicians Association (MTA) and who agree to adhere to the MTA Code of Ethics. Individuals with the CMT designation have demonstrated expertise in the field of technical analysis. Often CMTs will work for hedge funds and management firms.

The National Association of Estate Planners and Councils grants the *accredited estate planner* (AEP) credential to eligible planners, typically lawyers, who successfully complete two graduate courses through the American College. Advanced estate planning is required as well as an elective course related to estate planning.

How Advisors Can Add Value for You

A common question I hear is, "Are financial advisors worth their cost?" The range of cost for a financial advisor is between 0.75 percent and 1.5 percent of the investment portfolio. The typical fee is 1 percent for client assets of $1 million. A competent advisor should be providing suitable asset allocation that helps you meet your needs. He should also be providing cost-effective implementation and managing the expense ratios.

If you follow the advice of a qualified and experienced financial advisor who follows strict disciplines, she can potentially add much more in value over time than her fees cost. How do financial advisors do this?

- *Cost Effectiveness*—Managing investments in a cost-effective way by keeping expense ratios down. Your advisor could lower the average portfolio cost by 0.45 percent per year according to a recent study.[15]

- *Rebalancing*—Rebalancing is a key task to manage risk and add value. As I discussed earlier, rebalancing helps you keep your risk/return profile consistent. The value added to the average client's portfolio is estimated to be 0.35 percent per year.

- *Behavioral Coaching*—An advisor can manage your investments within your risk thresholds and help you make smarter financial choices. Often, having a good sounding board with an experienced and knowledgeable financial advisor can help you avoid making wrong decisions at the wrong time. This has actually been shown to have a very large impact of 1.5 percent per year for the average investor.

- *Asset Location*—An advisor can optimize where you locate specific types of investments to minimize your taxes. He can also help you structure your accounts in a tax-efficient manner. This can save a tremendous amount of money; on average, it is estimated to represent between 0 percent and 0.75 percent per year.

- *Withdrawal Strategies*—How you spend your money when it is time to take income and the order in which withdrawals are taken out of specific accounts can have a big impact on your results. Making withdrawals from the correct accounts at the correct time can add another 0.70 percent in returns per year.

- *Total-Return Investing*—Another valuable strategy is to manage your investment with a *total-return approach*. Instead of focusing only on the income generated from investments, a total-return approach blends capital growth, dividends, and interest in a way to seek better after-tax returns. Having the ability to look at the global picture, including capital gains and income, to reach a return objective can help a client over time.

The Value Equation for a Fiduciary Financial Advisor

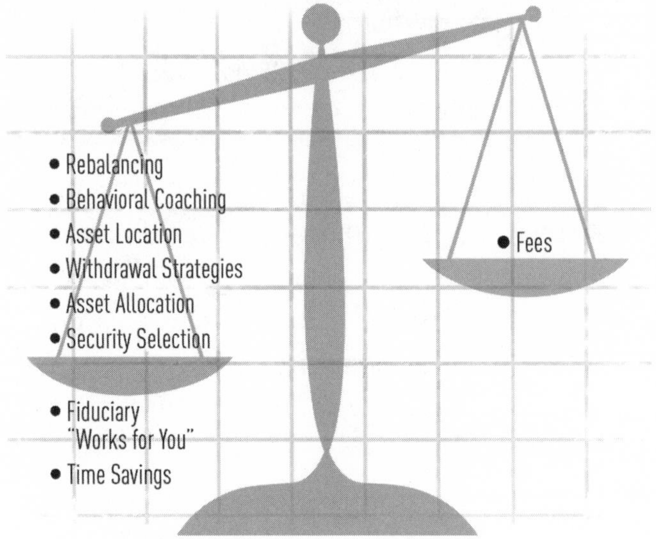

If you add all of these savings up, they total to between 3 percent and 3.75 percent. Of course, past performance is not necessarily indicative of future results, and investment returns cannot be guaranteed. You can see over time that investment performance can be dramatically improved by working with a competent advisor employed by a reputable fiduciary firm.

Also, do not forget that your time is valuable. If you are able to save a lot of time by working with a qualified, knowledgeable person, the value stacks up and improves your quality of life.

Don’t cut corners on expert advice.

A good financial advisor will charge a fee.

This allows them to consistently serve you and deliver results over time.

Advisor Checklist

Your advisor should be able to do the following to help you achieve financial independence:

- Optimize your cash flows to be more productive, and direct funds to improve the growth potential for your future.

- Use powerful strategies to lower your taxes by deducting, deferring, or avoiding taxes altogether.

- Develop a durable strategy to guide your personal asset allocation and to follow procedures to monitor and evaluate your holdings so that your advisor can make changes when appropriate.

- Stress-test your portfolio to see how reliable its growth could be during rough economic conditions.

- Harness the power of time-tested approaches for managing investments by practicing a systematic approach.

- Provide technology that you can access in a secure way to organize and track your entire financial picture so you can stay within your plan.

- Guarantee the quality of your financial plan and the service that your advisor delivers to you.

For regulatory reasons, your advisor cannot guarantee investment performance, but she should guarantee the quality of service. She should give you a clear path to achieve financial freedom.

Ten Key Questions to Ask Your Financial Advisor

Before you establish a relationship with a financial advisor, you'll want to interview several people to find one that is the right match for you. The Financial Planning Association suggests ten important questions you should ask before selecting a financial advisor:

1. What experience do you have?

Ask for a brief description of the financial advisor's work experience and how it relates to his current practice.

Professionals must have a minimum amount of experience to be able to understand how to work with you.

2. What are your qualifications?

Ask about the credentials that your advisor holds and learn about how she stays up to date with current changes, all the developments that are occurring in the markets, and financial planning issues. She should be expanding her knowledge by staying up to date and taking mandatory educational courses.

3. What financial planning services do you offer?

Credentials, licenses, and areas of expertise are all factors that determine the services a financial advisor can offer. Generally, financial advisors cannot sell insurance, security products, or mutual funds or stocks without proper licenses, and they cannot give investment advice unless registered with the state or federal authorities.

4. What is your approach to financial planning?

Make sure that the investment advisor has an investment philosophy and that you understand it. Make sure that it is neither too cautious nor overly aggressive for your needs. Learn how she will carry out recommendations or refer tasks to others.

5. What types of clients do you typically work with?

Some advisors prefer to work with clients whose assets fall within a particular range, so it's important to make sure that the advisor is a good fit for your individual financial situation. Keep in mind that some advisors require that you have a certain net worth before offering services.

6. Will you be the only advisor working with me?

Some financial advisors work with their clients directly, and others have a team of people that work with clients. Ask who would handle your accounts, who would meet with you, and whether the advisor works with professionals outside her practice, such as attorneys, insurance agents, or tax specialists. If she does, get a list of those professionals' names to check on their backgrounds.

7. How will I pay for your financial advisory services?

Advisors can be paid through fees, commissions, or a combination of both. As part of your written agreement, your advisor should make clear how she will be paid for the services to be provided.

8. How much do you typically charge?

Although what you will pay depends on your particular needs, the advisor should be able to provide you with an estimate of possible costs based on the work to be performed. Costs should include the advisor's hourly rates or flat fees, the percentage of assets under management, and/or commissions received on products you may purchase.

9. Do others stand to gain from the financial advice you give me?

Ask the advisor to provide you in writing with a description of his conflicts of interest. For example, a financial advisor who sells insurance policies, securities, and mutual funds for a commission will have business relationships with companies that provide those financial products.

CFA and CFP professionals both abide by strict codes of professional conduct and have an ethical obligation to put your needs above their own.

10. Have you ever been publicly disciplined for any unlawful or unethical actions in your career?

FINRA (the financial industry regulatory authority) and your state insurance and securities departments all keep records on the disciplinary history of financial advisors. Ask which organizations the advisor is regulated by, and contact those groups to conduct a background check.

It's important to understand what you can expect from your financial advisor. Here are some of the key traits recommended:

- *Competence*—A good advisor should be well-educated and able to demonstrate a significant amount of experience. Many individuals holding the CFA, CFP, and CPA designations are educated, tested, and experienced.

- *Objectivity*—Your needs should be at the heart of all of your advisor's recommendations. Your advisor should consider your situation carefully and give you advice that best meets your goals. This approach may require your advisor to explain that your goals are unrealistic given current resources and financial commitments.

- *Integrity*—Trust is central to a successful financial planning relationship. You rely on your planner's honesty, professionalism, and abilities to achieve your goals. When you know your planner takes her financial planner duties and responsibilities seriously and places principles over personal gain, you can form a good working relationship.

- *Clarity*—Fair treatment means your advisor will clearly state what financial planning services will be provided, along with their costs. Your advisor will explain the risks associated with her financial recommendations, along with potential conflicts of interest. For example, does your advisor gain personally or financially from your purchase of a particular product or from the outcome of her suggested strategy?

- *Diligence*—Before engaging you as a client, your advisor will discuss your goals and objectives and will explain what you can expect from the relationship and services. Once your advisor has determined that she, her staff, and any networked and related professionals can assist you, the planner will make recommendations suitable for you. A diligent financial advisor will reasonably investigate the products or services she recommends and will closely supervise any staff working with you.

- *Compliance*—Your advisor will not provide investment advice or stock services unless she is properly qualified and licensed to do so as required by state or federal law. There are different licenses for different reasons. Broker-dealers work for their companies, make commissions on transactions, and have one set of licenses; a registered investment advisor charges fees for services and acts as a fiduciary with a different set of licenses.

- *Privacy*—To get the best results from your financial planning relationship, you need to divulge relevant personal and financial information to your financial planner on a regular basis. Your advisor will keep this information in confidence, only sharing it to conduct business on your behalf, with your consent, or when ordered to do so by the courts.

Common Questions 9

The answers I remember longest are the ones that answer questions that I didn't think of asking.

—Jonathan Kozol

Most people have similar questions when they start to get serious about financial planning. This chapter will answer the ones I most frequently receive.

How do I know when I'm financially independent?

Knowing when you are financially independent mainly depends on the following factors:

- the amount of income you need to support your lifestyle
- how long you expect to live
- the return on your investments

- how much your portfolio fluctuates in value
- your tax circumstances
- the rate of future inflation

Of course, the amount of spendable cash you need each year will directly affect how much money you need, but what is not as obvious is that your portfolio volatility can reduce your future income. You can have a portfolio with positive returns over the long haul, but if it is also highly volatile, your money will not last as long as it could. A higher return is important, but so is keeping volatility down.

Imagine a water hose filling a bucket that has a hole in the bottom. As long as the amount of liquid coming into the bucket is greater than the amount leaking out, you will have an abundant amount of water. Likewise, as long as the earnings from your portfolio are greater than the money spent on your lifestyle, you are financially independent. But there is a caveat. The hole in the bottom of your financial bucket grows and gets bigger, letting out more and more money over time because of inflation. The same dollar amount today will be worth a lot less in the future, so you'll need more money. Also, other "leaks" occur when taxes and fees are deducted.

Now suppose you shake the bucket around a lot, causing some of the water to spill on the ground. This shaking of the bucket is just like investment volatility. If your portfolio has excessive fluctuations, then, even though you are earning a decent return (there's still lots of water coming into the bucket), more shares need to be sold to support a given level of income. This hinders the growth of your money and, more importantly, slows your ability to recoup your wealth when the markets are temporarily down. Of course, your financial bucket will then run out of money quicker.

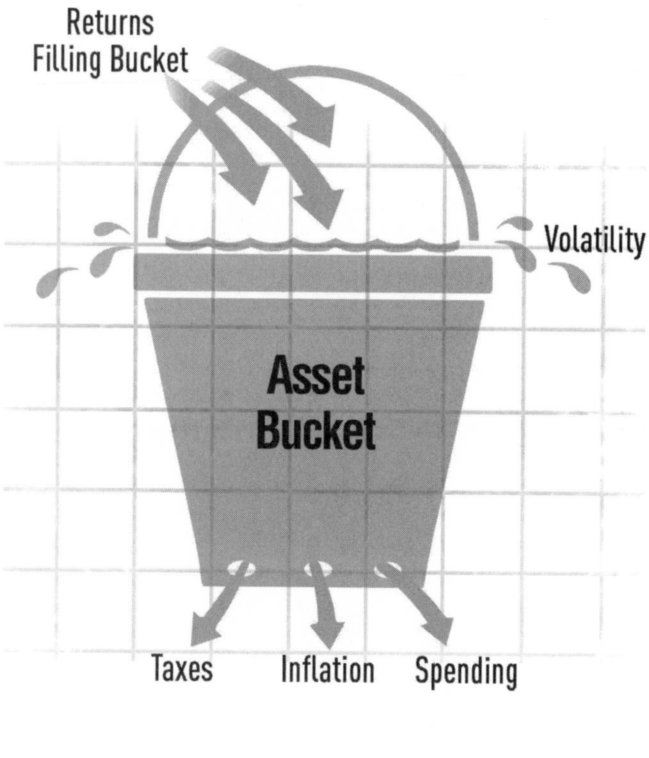

If you want your bucket to remain full for the rest of your life, you'll need enough money, a reasonably strong return with relatively low volatility, and a strategy to minimize taxes and fees.

The best way to figure out the size of your "personal bucket" is to create a financial plan. The planning process uses sophisticated software to estimate your spending needs in the future, how much you might pay in taxes, and the impact of inflation. The plan should also account for fluctuations that may be anticipated in your accounts. I usually recommend a Monte Carlo simulation that models your plan and runs thousands of iterations to see how often your plan is successful in meeting your goals.

The reason to create the plan is to identify ways to improve your investments, lower your taxes and fees, and make smart financial choices with your hard-earned income and assets. Going through this process should lead to actions that will maximize the effectiveness of your resources so you experience the life that you desire.

What information do I need to create a comprehensive financial plan?

You will need to gather some information to create a sound plan. First, you'll need factual figures in the following categories:

- assets
- liabilities
- income

- expenses
- family information

This will allow you to see your net worth and income statements, estimate your taxes, and build up your cash-flow forecasts. See the Document Checklist in the Appendix for a complete list of recommended items.

Goals and Aspirations

Ultimately, this requires an assessment of your personal values. You can't achieve your dreams if they are not first envisioned in your mind, but if you get a clear picture of them, you can take action to transform your situation.

Probably one of the hardest questions to answer is, "What do I really want out of life?" Happiness is a hard thing to quantify, but to make a good plan, you must dig deep inside yourself and decide what is important to you about money and life.

How much income can I withdraw from my investments each year?

To answer this question, it's best to consider your spending rate. The spending rate is the amount of money you can spend for the rest of your life. It is expressed as a percent of your total liquid portfolio value. For example, if you are taking an income of $80,000 per year on a $2,000,000 portfolio, your spending rate is 4.00 percent ($80,000 ÷ $2,000,000 = 4%).

Investment managers and academics have spent considerable time researching ways to find a sustainable spending rate, a rate at which an investor can spend money over a lifetime without running out of funds.

To stay wealthy, most people spend less than 2 percent of their money in any given year.

To estimate your personal spending rate, a good starting point is to calculate an actuarial rate based on your real return, the volatility of your portfolio, and your life expectancy. It is best to adjust your return downward to account for taxes that could be paid. This results in a real return after taxes. To help you answer this question, I have created a chart showing sustainable spending rates given the long-term history of market returns.

The chart is easy to use. Just find your age in the far-left column, and then look over to the spending rates based on your personal risk tolerance. For simplicity, I have limited the chart to three common types of investors: conservative, moderate, and aggressive. To calculate how much income you can spend per year, just multiply the spending rate times your portfolio value. For example, if your spending rate is 3 percent and your portfolio value is $1,000,000, you can take out $30,000 per year and inflate it in future years as the cost of living goes up. The calculations in the chart are based on a sophisticated actuarial model developed by Moshe Milevsky and Chris Robinson.[16]

Let's say you want to be financially independent at age fifty-five, you have a moderate risk tolerance, and you estimate that you will need an annual income of $100,000. This income will also need to go up with inflation over time so you don't lose your spending power. Based on the chart, your sustainable spending rate is 3.9 percent.

To calculate the amount of money you will need to have accumulated, simply divide your annual income need of $100,000 by 3.9 percent, which is $2,564,103. You will therefore need about $2.5 million to fund an annual spending power of $100,000, going up with inflation, for the rest of your life.

Table 2. Spending Rates (1) for Sustainable Income

Current Age	Remaining Lifespan (2)	Conservative	Moderate	Aggressive
45	35.78	3.3%	3.6%	3.4%
50	31.31	3.4%	3.7%	3.6%
55	27.03	3.6%	3.9%	3.8%
60	22.91	3.9%	4.1%	4.0%
65	18.94	4.2%	4.5%	4.4%
70	15.23	4.7%	4.9%	4.8%
75	11.85	5.4%	5.6%	5.6%
80	8.85	6.4%	6.7%	6.6%

Table 3. Historical Performance (3)

	Conservative	Moderate	Aggressive
Real Return	3.80%	4.80%	5.80%
Volatility	6.38%	9.53%	13.66%

1. Based on Milevsky Sustainable Spending Rate Model, using a 90 percent success rate.

2. Social Security Administration Life Tables.

3. Historical real returns and volatility from 1802–2006, Stocks for the Long Run, Jeremy Siegel.

It is important to note that an aggressive investor is not really able to spend more than a moderate risk-taker.

Why is that? The answer is that volatility causes less certainty and requires investors to be more cautious about the negative effects of reverse-dollar cost averaging.

Remember the bucket being jiggled around and water spilling out? This is why.

I want to live off my interest and dividends while leaving my principal alone. How do I invest in a portfolio of high-income securities?

Although spending interest and dividends alone sounds like a reasonable way to protect your principal, in reality it can be harmful to your wealth. To create the income needed, an investor must search for securities that pay higher dividends and interest. Doesn't that sound good?

There are a few problems, though, with this *income-only strategy*.

If you screen all the publicly-traded investments to include only those with the highest-paying income, you will have a list of companies concentrated in certain industries, typically oil and gas, telecommunication, real estate, and financial groups. This concentration increases your *sector risk*, which leaves your portfolio vulnerable to sharp declines when those industries run into hard times. Another problem is that stocks that pay higher dividends tend to grow at a much slower pace than the overall market. Why is this? Because companies that pay out a high dividend to investors tend to be in mature, slow-growing industries with a limited number of new investment projects that might increase future growth. Does it really make sense to concentrate investments in slow growers?

Let's switch gears to bonds as opposed to stocks. Why not focus on those bonds that pay higher interest? To get higher income from bonds, you usually need to invest more money in issuers with lower-quality credit ratings.

These issuers have a higher chance of missing interest and principal payments in the future, especially if the economy weakens. As a result, prices are much more volatile, and they perform like stocks. Second, investors have to buy bonds with longer-term maturities to get higher income. This subjects the investor to *interest rate* or *duration risk* because these investments' price movements are very sensitive to changes in market interest rates.

Longer-term bonds will fall much more rapidly than short-term bonds if interest rates rise.

You might be wondering, "If an income-only strategy is not ideal, then what is a better way to generate lifetime income?"

I recommend a *total-return approach*. This strategy incorporates all sources of returns, including capital gains, dividends, and interest, as opposed to relying ONLY on interest and dividends for income.

Studies have shown that investors achieve better returns, more diversification, and lower tax bills as a result of a total-return approach. A total-return portfolio is constructed by diversifying across distinct types of assets that have very few overlapping fundamentals. I also advise investors to diversify among different styles within each type of asset. Adding absolute-return managers to your mix could also reduce risk.

My insurance agent or financial advisor is recommending an annuity to fund my retirement. Does this make sense for me?

A complete answer to this question requires specific information about your policy and your own unique circumstances. There are many types of annuity policies.

In some cases, they can add tremendous advantages, but in many cases, there are pitfalls to avoid. Here are some of the pros and cons of fixed and variable annuities:

Pros

- They can provide stability of principal and guaranteed returns.

- You can annuitize the policy to provide guaranteed income for the rest of your life. If you live longer than expected, you will still receive income and you cannot run out of money.

- Earnings from the investment can be sheltered from taxation until you withdraw funds. This allows for tax-deferred compounding that is similar to a retirement account, such as an IRA.

- Some equity-index annuities allow for participation in stock-market gains while guaranteeing the principal.

Cons

- Fixed annuities can lose purchasing power because their rates of return have historically been lower than those of stocks, real estate, and some alternative investments.

- Market participation rates of equity-index annuities are low and are limited when the stock markets have large gains; be cautious about expecting large gains while limiting losses. There is no free lunch, and there are levers that insurance companies pull that may not be obvious.

- Your funds may be locked up, requiring large penalty payments if you withdraw money.

- If you take money out before age fifty-nine and a half, the gains are taxed as income, not capital gains. For many people this increases taxes.

- Some variable annuities are riddled with large fees, such as mortality costs, fund expenses, rider costs, hidden commissions, and other administration fees.

- If you pass an annuity on to heirs, there is no step-up in the cost basis to eliminate capital gains; therefore, your heirs will pay income taxes when using the funds.

Annuities are a tool for financial security but are not all created equal. Beware of complex annuities used for the wrong reasons.

Other Tips

Here are some general tips to see if an annuity might make sense for you:

- If you are in a high tax bracket and are already maxing out retirement plans, but you still need tax relief, annuities can certainly help.

- If you are still growing your money and want additional tax-deferred growth, invest in low-cost no-load variable annuities that do not have penalties. This will allow you to have more liquidity and flexibility with your annuity, with lower fees to increase your potential returns.

- If you are risk averse and want principal protection, a fixed annuity with guaranteed returns can provide stability and tax deferral.

- If you want protection against running out of income during retirement, you can annuitize or invest in a single-premium income annuity to get an income stream for life. Consider setting up your income plan to pay a minimum number of payments regardless of how long you live to ensure that your heirs will get back all of your money plus interest. Otherwise, your family could lose out if you unexpectedly die early.

- Be sure you have adequate liquid investments that are not in IRAs or other retirement plans. This gives you more flexibility to access funds without paying penalties or income tax on withdrawals.

- Consult with a knowledgeable, experienced advisor to see if an annuity makes sense. Make sure the advisor is not motivated by selling high-margin products that may not be in your best interests.

I've changed jobs and have a 401(k) at my previous employer. Should I roll it over into an IRA?

You can do four things with a retirement plan from your old employer:

1. cash it out;
2. leave it in your old employer's plan;
3. roll it over to your new employer's plan; or
4. roll it over to an IRA.

Let's start with option one: cashing it out. As long as you don't cash out your IRA, you don't pay taxes, but if you do take possession of your IRA before the age of fifty-nine and a half, you'll pay dearly. Early redemption will cost you a 10 percent penalty, plus the withdrawn funds are fully taxable as income. Talk about expensive! If you are in the middle tax bracket, you will pay an additional 28 percent in income taxes, totaling 38 percent that is sent out the door to the Internal Revenue Service. For this reason, cashing out is usually not a smart choice.

Options two and three, leaving it in your old employer's plan or rolling it over to your new employer's plan, both require an analysis of each plan's investment options and fees. In order for either of these choices to make sense, the plan must have a very strong line-up of fund options and low fees. The plans must give you the flexibility similar to the option of rolling it over into a self-directed 401(k). Usually this is not the case.

Upon evaluating the retirement plans of many clients, I have found them to lack the robust options that are required to construct a strong portfolio. This leaves investors vulnerable to the general volatility of the stock and bond markets with few options other than cash and short-term fixed income as a refuge.

Here are some reasons why this occurs:

- Employers tend to limit their investment selections to 401(k), 403(b), and other retirement plans, because they need to monitor and keep in strict compliance with regulations.

- If the employer has too many options in the plan, there is less participation in each fund by employees. As the number of funds increases, fewer employees invest enough in each of the funds to justify the costs to the company. The company needs to have strong participation to pay for the plan and to minimize its own costs.

- Companies have limited choices because they have a fiduciary liability. They are liable for the investments made within the investment plan. So, to mitigate their liability, they generally use fewer funds because it's less costly to be compliant.

Your retirement plan at work probably does not cover all the types of investments you need to have healthy returns in good times and bad.

They are stuck with traditional investments in stocks, bonds, and cash. There are usually no alternatives or other subclasses that historically have been strong diversifiers.

The fees in your 401(k) could also affect your decision to roll it over to an IRA. According to AARP, 67 percent of employees think that they have no fees in their 401(k) plans. This is just false. Participants should understand what those fees are. Embedded in your retirement plan are record-keeping, third-party administrative, custodial, and advisory fees. On top of those fees, don't forget the expense ratios of the funds in the line-up. Most investors do not see these fees, but they are very real. Sometimes plans can be bundled or unbundled. These costs may be passed on to the employer or the employees, so you have to check the plan out.

In my experience, most employees benefit from rolling over their old 401(k) plans into self-directed IRAs at reputable brokerage firms. This gives them full access to a plethora of investment choices with very competitive fee structures and responsive service. Companies like Charles Schwab, Fidelity, and TD Ameritrade give you access to thousands of funds with no loads and no transaction fees. You also can invest in exchange-traded funds, stocks, bonds, options, and other securities while paying low commissions.

I want to retire before age fifty-nine and a half, but I have most of my money in retirement accounts. What can I do?

There are special provisions in the Internal Revenue Code that allow you to take income from your retirement accounts before the age of fifty-nine and a half without paying penalties! You must follow specific rules in IRC Section 72(q) and 72(t) to qualify for this exemption.

These provisions state that you must withdraw substantially equal periodic payments that are calculated using one of three methods:

- minimum distribution method
- amortization method
- annuitization method

As long as you follow the rules, there are no penalties; however, you still have to pay income tax on the withdrawals. Be sure to consult your CPA or tax advisor to verify that your calculations are correct; otherwise, you may pay penalties.

Should I max out my 401(k)?

This is a very complicated question because many things are unknown.

To make a smart choice, consider the following questions:

- What percentage of your assets is currently held in liquid taxable assets?
- What is your current income and tax bracket?
- Does your company match your contributions?
- Do you expect tax rates to increase or decrease in the future?

To keep your money safe, your returns must exceed taxes, inflation, and your spending.

A steady investment strategy can keep you secure for the rest of your life and beyond.

Once you have answered those questions, then consider the following guidelines:

1. It is recommended that you first make sure you have enough liquid taxable assets to have an adequate reserve before you invest for retirement.

2. If your company matches your contributions up to a certain percentage of your salary, you probably should at least contribute that percentage, because you will be earning a 100 percent return on each dollar.

3. If you have goals that require the use of your money before you retire, then you should invest those funds outside of your retirement accounts.

4. If you've met the first three guidelines, and if you have enough income left over, then you probably should max out your retirement account.

The best way to get clear on this question is to run a complete financial plan. This will give you a more detailed look at your options so you can determine which strategy is best for your specific situation.

Max out your retirement savings if possible, but make sure you have liquid protection outside your retirement money.

Are mutual funds a good investment from a tax perspective?

Mutual funds have the potential to spin off taxes to investors in a way that is very unpleasant. This unpleasant tax is called the *phantom tax*. The phantom tax occurs when an investor buys into a fund that has already accumulated gains.

If the fund managers decide to realize gains accrued prior to your investments, a portion of those gains will apply to you, even though you did not earn the gain!

It is possible that you actually have a loss in the investments from the moment you entered the fund; because those prior gains were already there, they are sent out to you, an existing shareholder at the time of the realized gain, on a prorated basis.

This phantom tax is quite annoying, but thankfully, it can be avoided. Investing in exchange-traded funds is a good alternative. ETFs can be more tax efficient; compared to traditional mutual funds, there are fewer taxable events. Here's why. A conventional mutual fund must constantly rebalance the fund by selling securities to accommodate shareholder redemptions or to reallocate assets. The sale of securities within the mutual-fund portfolio creates capital gains for current, not previous, shareholders.

In contrast, an ETF manager accommodates investment inflows and outflows by creating or redeeming creation units, which are baskets of assets that approximate the entirety of the ETF investment exposure. As a result, the investors usually are not exposed to capital gains on any individual security in the underlying structure.

How can I manage the downside risk in my portfolio?

You want to establish a risk profile that considers your tolerance and capacity for taking risk. You then translate your profile into a *risk budget* that defines the drawdown and standard deviation that are acceptable. Establish an asset allocation policy that is congruent with your risk profile, then manage the size of investments so you remain within your risk requirements.

This process requires diversification among asset classes and strategies within the markets with a keen eye toward the correlation of and relationships between constituents in your portfolio. The correlation between investments tends to rise during periods of market stress. This means many investments go down in value at the same time. So how do we mitigate this? By allocating capital into alternative strategies that have absolute-return objectives.

An *absolute-return objective* means that investment managers have a mandate to try to make money whether the market is going up or down. The manager is not restricted to trying to follow a benchmark like the S&P 500 or the Barclays Aggregate Bond Index. Instead, they seek to make profits regardless of market direction. Also, look for alternative strategies that participate in a broad range of investments, including stocks, bonds, commodities, and currencies.

You want to make sure that the managers of the alternative strategies that you are investing in also have the ability to make a profit regardless of the market's direction. These managers can make profits when the market is going up by buying investments, and they can make money when a market goes down by shorting an investment.

Pre-defining risk *before* investing and diversification are the two greatest tools to make the most money for a given level of risk.

Avoidable Ten Mistakes 10

Mistakes are inevitable. The key to big mistakes is only making them once.

—Jeffrey Gitomer

With a successful career in full bloom, and a busy lifetime spent working towards goals, it is common to forget to plan for "what comes next." In this frantic and fast-paced life, it is normal not to have enough time to plan one of the most important and complex decisions in our life. A highly-functioning, effective retirement plan can allow us to enjoy retirement for decades.

The Cost of Being Too Busy

There are a lot of reasons why effective retirement planning is important for executives who have dedicated so many years of their lives nurturing their career. When time, energy, and effort have been spent towards successfully achieving financial goals, it's critical to take care of your nest egg. To retire comfortably, and to fulfill your life's dreams in the best way, we need a plan.

One of the reasons planning for retirement is so important is because it can last a lot longer than you think.

According to the Social Security Administration, most people will live past their eightieth birthday, meaning that retirement could last over twenty-five years. In addition, recent studies also indicate that 80 percent of today's sixty-five-year-olds will need long-term supportive care, making it imperative to have your finances in check to ensure a brighter future. If you are well prepared, then this is great news; who wouldn't want to enjoy the retirement life they've dreamt of? However, if your retirement planning isn't adequate, living longer can quickly turn into a worrisome condition.

Many executives looking towards their future commonly make ten mistakes that are very dangerous for the health and wellness of their finances, especially in later years. Implementing an effective retirement plan can help avoid these mistakes, maximize your investments, and increase resources so you can keep living the lifestyle you desire for the rest of your life. The good news is these mistakes can be avoided.

Mistake One: Making Decisions without Considering Loved Ones

It goes without saying that everybody wants the future to be the most secure and carefree time of their lives to spend with family. When making retirement plan decisions, many executives often don't fully consider the impact these important financial decisions will have on their spouse, family, children, and even grandchildren. When considering solutions to make your retirement years enjoyable, discuss the financial goals with the important people in your life to ensure that all aspects are considered and appropriately addressed.

Mistake Two: An Improper View of Your Net Worth

With family and work demands, time may not allow you to organize all aspects of your finances to take proper inventory of where you stand. However, knowing your net worth is fundamental to organizing a proper retirement plan. The number-one way to do this is to look at your financial picture with a comprehensive, unbiased analysis of your current strengths, opportunities, and dangers.

Some common pitfalls include:

- not properly valuing and accounting for all assets and liabilities

- not fully considering the necessary cash reserve and liquidity needs
- not knowing the location and titling of your assets
- not being aware of ways to save money on taxes with various account types

Everything needs to be considered and thoroughly analyzed to optimize your net worth to your advantage.

Mistake Three: Not Considering the Timing of All Income Sources

Income sources often change over time. For example, Social Security, required minimum distributions, pensions, and rental property income will likely vary during your lifetime. Having a holistic view of all your income sources, both now and in the future, will help you have a better understanding of your cash-flow needs. Clearly understanding the timing and expectation of income are critically necessary for avoiding cash-flow mistakes.

Mistake Four: Underestimating the Cost of Taxes, Healthcare, and Debt

Being able to run a proper analysis of expenses is key when organizing a retirement plan. Consider taxes; they have a significant impact on your life, from the quality of the lifestyle you can lead, to the ability to pursue your goals. This is why comprehensive tax planning is crucial to your financial health.

Managing debt and rising healthcare costs are also a big consideration. Proper debt management can significantly improve your ability to have financial independence.

Healthcare costs are quickly rising, and inflation should be taken into consideration while making plans. Recent studies state that healthcare is expected to add $300,000 in ancillary costs per family—and that's in today's dollars! In the future, this sum will inevitably reach a higher ceiling, and this makes forecasting and analyzing expenses imperative.

Mistake Five: Not Setting Clear Priorities

How do you prioritize retirement when there's so much to think about, like the education of your children, taking care of a parent, buying cars, paying down debt, and enjoying life today with travel and fun? This may seem counterintuitive, but the truth is, life needs balance, and finding it is challenging. More often than we would like, retirement planning decisions come down to a trade-off between living well now and having abundance for future years. Prioritization is key to make sure everything has its space in our finances, both in the present and in the future!

Not being able to see the future and what your wants and needs will be can be difficult. With that said, setting proper goals requires you to estimate the timing and amount of funds you need. Because this can be difficult, it's easy to see why having a nebulous goal isn't something that will take you far. It's absolutely critical to have a properly-defined objective and to be able to estimate how much money you will need to turn your dreams into a solid reality.

Setting specific goals requires you to question your values. Ask yourself, "What is important about money to me?" Also ask yourself, "Why is this important to me?" Having an advisor as a sounding board can be very helpful during this process; and don't forget to include your spouse or significant people in your life. Having a comprehensive, results-oriented retirement plan is vital in setting yourself up to live life comfortably.

Mistake Seven: Inefficient Savings

Financial security can be achieved faster and easier when you save and contribute in an efficient manner. Because there are so many different types of investments with various risks and returns, making sound choices to optimize your savings can help you build more wealth.

Many executives may need assistance in strategically using their employer plan to their best advantage.

The mix of stocks, bonds, cash, and various asset classes that make up your finances is essential. Since each element of the mix has different returns and risks, the management of your investments is a rather meticulous endeavor.

A sound investment plan should consider your return requirements, risk tolerance, liquidity and income needs, taxes, personal preferences, and any special circumstances. Most importantly, your investment plan must be aligned with your financial plan. Having a holistic view and a good understanding of asset allocation is required in order to achieve the goals you have set for your future.

Mistake Nine: Not Protecting Your Money

Managing the unexpected things in life, both before and after your retirement date, is fundamental for financial security.

Having adequate financial protection can help you live a more healthy, stress-free life. Unfortunately, executives may overlook or underestimate needed protection during retirement for life, health, and more commonly, long-term care. A good retirement plan should help you identify risks and develop affordable ways to mitigate them so that your plans are not derailed by unforeseen events. Healthcare costs are underestimated more often than not, and the major risk this brings us is having to face unexpected issues completely unprepared financially.

Mistake Ten: Lack of Monitoring and Adjusting

Last, but certainly not least, not monitoring your progress and adjusting over time may very well be the biggest mistake when it comes to planning your future. Establishing a timely, periodic review and staying on track can have a huge impact on your success. To keep yourself on track, and to be able to make smart choices about your finances, you need to continuously track, monitor, and observe your situation. One element that is constantly changing and needs to be addressed is the economy. Typically, changes in the economy affect your taxes, cost of living, the return on your investments, and risks. As your life changes, your retirement plan may change and require adjustment based on unexpected issues, necessities, and even new goals.

Proper portfolio construction requires more than just a questionnaire. There are many factors that go into designing a portfolio that is optimal for you. Make sure you have the information necessary to select the investment strategy you believe has the best opportunity of meeting your goals and objectives. For example, understanding your income tax bracket, current and future income sources—such as Social Security, pension, or rental income—as well as any real estate or business interest plays a critical role in designing the portfolio best suited to meet your unique needs.

If you decided to work with an advisor, consider their experience and credentials. Are they required by law to always act in your best interest as a fiduciary? Do they work with a team that will include experienced Chartered Financial Analysts (CFAs), financial planning practitioners, and other credentialed advisors?

Here are the main things to find out:

- Are portfolios tailored to my unique needs?
- Are fees transparent and simple?
- Are there any conflicts of interest?

Be sure to refer to Chapter 8, "Choose the Right Advisors," for more information on this topic.

Putting It All Together 11

The object of all work is production or accomplishment and to either of these ends there must be forethought, system, planning, intelligence, and honest purpose, as well as perspiration.

—Thomas A. Edison

I discussed the crucial steps to effective planning: identifying and prioritizing your objectives, gathering your data, analyzing the data, evaluating your alternatives, creating an investment policy statement, implementing your plan, and putting a monitoring system in place.

I discussed powerful tax-reducing strategies that can help you build wealth quicker: how you can optimize contributions to tax-deferred and tax-free accounts; use better tax-lot accounting methods with tax-loss harvesting and replacement; invest in municipal bonds when it makes sense; avoid the phantom tax and other unnecessary taxes; locate your assets in the right accounts so you have the right asset-allocation strategy and pay less in taxes; and manage your withdrawal strategy to give you the best results.

Last, I discussed asset allocation and security selection. We saw how an evidence-based approach can help you control risk, diversify properly, invest for absolute return, and rebalance your portfolio.

These tactics can help you minimize errors and avoid costly mistakes. Take action today on what you've discovered.

Just decide to make it happen.

Look forward to the possible, not backward to irrelevant history.

Appendix

GOAL-GRADING WORKSHEET

GOAL DESC-RIPTION	URGENCY	PEOPLE	PASSIONS	HEALTH	SPIRITUAL	SOCIETY	TOTAL

My most important, number-one goal is:

My number-two goal is:

My number-three goal is:

My number-four goal is:

My number-five goal is:

____

____

____

DOCUMENT CHECKLIST

You will need the following documents to prepare a comprehensive financial plan:

- Risk-assessment questionnaire
- Most recent W-2
- Most recent tax return
- Taxable account statements:
    - CDs, money market accounts, and other cash equivalents
    - Brokerage accounts
    - Other accounts
- Employer retirement account statements and plan information:
    - Social Security Statement (Estimate of Benefits)

  - Pensions
  - 401(k) account information
  - Other employer information
  - Other retirement account statements
  - Annuities (policies and statements)
  - Traditional and Roth IRAs
  - Deferred compensation
- College account statements:
  - 529
  - UTMA/UGMA
  - Other
- Insurance policies and statement information:
  - Cash-value life insurance (whole life, universal, variable, other)
  - Term insurance
  - Long-term care

- Disability
- Real Estate
    - Rental properties
    - Estimated value
- Estimated cash flow
- Trust documents
- Stock option and restricted stock statements and plan information
- Personal and business assets:
    - Estimated market value of home, land, and other personal property
    - Estimated market value of business and expected cash flows
- Liabilities:
    - Mortgage balances, interest rates, and payments
    - Other debt balances, interest rates, and payments

The best way to view your finances is in a holistic fashion, putting it all together and looking at it in its entirety. This vantage point will give you the best chance to make smart financial choices.

Acknowledgments

I want to thank and acknowledge the many people that have shaped my thinking and the contents of this book. First, I'd like to acknowledge Dan Sullivan, whose tremendous work through Strategic Coach has spurred ideas to provide value for clients, and how to leverage my firm's people with unique ability teamwork. Second, I'd like to thank Jeffrey Gitomer, who taught me to cultivate creativity and to incorporate humor in my work. His mastery of wordsmith capabilities is truly a gift. His advice and approach have been instrumental in helping me write this book. I'd also like to thank Jennifer Gitomer, who subtly provided dynamite ideas in the process of writing.

The financial analysis work of Moshe A. Milveski, a leading authority in education at the Schulich School of Business, York University, was used in analytical models utilized by my firm. His contribution to retirement income planning has been groundbreaking and served as a foundation for sustainable withdrawal rates in this book.

I'd like to thank Ralph Acampora, the former Director of Technical Analysis at Prudential Securities. He taught me, after a panel discussion together, that there is a big difference between the fundamentals of a company and the stock of a company. The company stock price often leads the fundamentals and can diverge from Wall Street's view. This concept has helped my firm manage risk and make money over the years.

Robert Carver, a great quantitative analyst, and author of *Systematic Trading*, has influenced ideas through his writings, especially regarding portfolio construction and position sizing. I want to thank the CPAs we have worked with over the years, particularly Steve Haskins, CPA, and James Wallace, CPA, whose work on stock options and complicated stock scenarios with our clients has shaped our advice regarding company stock. Thank you, Katherine Kaminski, who introduced the concept of convergent and divergent strategies. This has added another dimension to our asset allocation.

I also want to acknowledge Maclyn Clouse, PhD, a professor when I attended the Graduate School at the University of Denver. He proposed the concept of "the value you give up versus the value you get." This financial thinking has helped me solve many challenges facing clients.

There are many people in the trading world that have influenced my philosophy. I want to thank Richard Rines, Cesar Alvarez, and Alex Sun, CFA, CMT, who did extensive programming, quantitative analysis, and trading system design for my firm.

I also want to thank Jason Meshnick at IHS Markit for his creativity and ability to pull out ideas from me. His work about volume in stocks has been very useful and practical for managing assets for clients. I'd like to also thank James Smith, a long-term colleague who urged me to be more skeptical about messages received by the media and politicians. Van Tharpe's work and writings have contributed to my thinking about investor psychology in this book. This has helped me align investor psychology with useful beliefs to leverage performance. Michael Carr, an excellent investment newsletter writer, has been a great help to me with his writing tips. I still strive to communicate ideas based on his advice. I also want to acknowledge Pam Fogel for her graphical artwork and Mike Wolff for his contributions to the design of the inside of this book. Thank you to my family who supported me and provided great ideas along the way.

Finally, I want to thank Rabbi Richard Rheins, Rabbi Jordy Callman, and Rabbi Avraham Mintz for their spiritual guidance in my life.

Smart planning backed by data can increase your success exponentially.

About the Author

Louis B. Llanes is the founder of Wealthnet Investments, LLC. Louis leads strategy and vision for the firm and serves on the investment committee. Louis also advises key clients of the firm.

In 1997, Louis founded Blythe Lane Investment Management and later merged the firm with Centric Investment Group, which later became Wealthnet Investments, LLC. He also served as a senior portfolio manager for the US Bank Private Client Reserve, a quantitative trader for a private fund, and an investment consultant for Kemper Securities.

Early in his career, he worked as a financial analyst for Intellogic Trace, a spin-off of DataPoint, and a Quantitative Analyst. Louis holds the Chartered Financial Analyst (CFA) and Chartered Market Technician (CMT) designations. He earned an MBA at the University of Denver and a BS in Finance from the University of Colorado in Denver.

Louis is the author of *Financial Freedom Blueprint*, a contributing author in *The Handbook of Risk*, and has written white papers about investment management issues for practitioners. Louis has held chair positions on the board for the Colorado chapter of the Institute for Chartered Financial Analyst and Chartered Market Technician Association based in New York.

Endnotes

1 Kahneman, Daniel, and Amos Tversky. "Prospect Theory: An Analysis of Decision Under Risk." *Econometrica*, vol. 47, no. 2 (March 1979): 263–92. http://www.jstor.org/stable/1914185?seq=1#page_scan_tab_contents.

2 Llanes, Louis B. "Converging Correlation and Market Shocks." In *The Handbook of Risk*, edited by Ben Warwick, 189–206. Hoboken, NJ: John Wiley, 2003.

3 Fama, Eugene, and Kenneth French. "A Five-Factor Asset Pricing Model." Social Science Research Network. (September 23, 2014): http://papers.ssrn.com/sol3/papers.cfm?abstract_id=2287202.

4 Asness, Clifford, Andrea Frazzini, Ronen Israel, and Tobias Moskowitz. "Fact, Fiction and Momentum Investing." *Journal of Portfolio Management,* Vol. 40, no. 5 (May 12, 2014): 75–92. https://www.aqr.com/-/media/AQR/Documents/Insights/Interviews/PA--Fact-Fiction-and-Momentum-Investing-FINAL.pdf.

5 Moskowitz, Tobias, Yao Hua Ooi, and Lasse Heje Pedersen. "Time Series Momentum." *Journal of Financial Economics*, vol. 104, no. 2 (May 2012): 228–50. http://www.sciencedirect.com/science/article/pii/S0304405X11002613.

6 Bernicke, Ty. "The Real Cost of Owning a Mutual Fund." *Forbes*. (April 4, 2011): http://www.forbes.com/2011/04/04 /real-cost-mutual-fund-taxes-fees-retirement-bernicke.html.

7 Ibid.

8 Du, Jianan, Janis Zvingelis, and Brandon Thomas. "Active vs. Passive Asset Management." Envestnet. (2015): 1–7. http://www.envestnet.com/sites/default/files/documents/PMC-AP-0114-WhitePaper.pdf.

9 Ibid.

10 Dichtl, Hubert, Wolfgang Drobetz, and Martin Wambach. "Where Is the Value Added of Rebalancing? A Systematic Comparison of Alternative Rebalancing Strategies." Social Science Research Network. (February 4, 2014): http://papers.ssrn.com/sol3/papers.cfm?abstract_id=2139915.

11 Congressional Budget Office. "Updated Budget Projections: 2015 to 2025." (March 9, 2015): 5. https://www.cbo.gov/ publication /49973.

12 US Department of the Treasury. "The Debt to the Penny and Who Holds It." https://fiscaldata.treasury.gov/datasets/debt-to-the-penny/debt-to-the-penny.

13 Vanguard. "Putting a Value on Your Value: Quantifying Vanguard Advisor's Alpha." (March 10, 2014): https://advisors.vanguard.com/VGApp/iip/site/advisor/researchcommentary/article/IWE_InvResValueAdvisorsAlpha.

14 Ibid.

15 Ibid.

16 Milevsky, Moshe and Chris Robinson. "A Sustainable Spending Rate Without Simulation." *Financial Analysts Journal*, vol. 61, no. 6 (November/December 2005): 89–100.